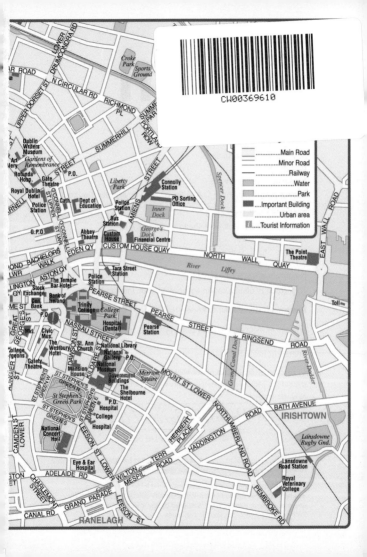

Dublin

Text: Howard Rose, & Bernice Mulligan
Text Editor: Emma Meade
Cartography: Global Mapping Ltd
Advertising: James Small
Design: John Barrett
Production: Emma Meade
Photography: Irish Image Collection, www.irishimagecollection.com

Publishing Information:
This 12th edition was published October 2014 by:
Select Media Ltd.,
26 Clare Street, Dublin 2
Tel: +353 1 6622266
Email: info@selectmedialtd.com
This guide is distributed in association with Tourism Ireland

Publishers: Denis Lane & Robert Heuston

Typeset in Meta and ATRotis Serif 55
ISBN: 1-904895-01-8
Printed in Ireland

Premier Guides Ltd

If you have any questions, queries or suggestions we'd be delighted to hear your
contributions for the next edition. Please send to info@selectmedialtd.com

CONTENTS

Christchurch bells
The book of Kells
A trip to Howth
And fishy smells

DART hits the spot

GUINNESS STOREHOUSE - THE HOME OF GUINNESS

Every capital city has its iconic buildings and 'must-see' attractions. **Guinness**® is synonymous with Ireland and when in Dublin, no visit is complete without a trip to **Guinness Storehouse**®.

Guinness Storehouse is Ireland's number one visitor attraction located in the heart of the Guinness Brewery at St James's Gate. Housed in an old fermentation plant, the seven-storey visitor experience brings to life the rich heritage of Guinness telling the story from its origins here at St. James's Gate in Dublin to its growth as a global brand, know all around the world.

Your journey through Guinness Storehouse takes you on a story Made of More that begins over 255 years ago. Enjoy a sensory experience in our Tasting Rooms, learn how to craft the perfect pint at Guinness Academy, try our delicious Guinness and Food offerings, and take in the spectacular views of Dublin city from Gravity Bar.

Top Tip: Book your tickets online in advance at www.guinness-storehouse.com to receive a 10% discount off adult tickets and to skip the queue on arrival.

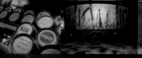

Ha'penny Bridge, River Liffey

Today's Dublin is a swirling mixture of energy, culture and excitement. Originally a small Viking settlement (its name comes from 'Dubh Linn', meaning dark pool) and then, for many years, a British stronghold, Dublin has once more undergone a complete metamorphosis and is now one of Europe's hottest capitals.

A quick look around will confirm how this once insular, monocultural city has transformed itself into a fantastic destination for tourists, students, writers and musicians. Immigration has brought people from every destination imaginable to live and work in Dublin, giving the city a decidedly cosmopolitan air. Thousands more flood the capital at weekends for literary festivals, sporting events, bridal and grooms parties, or simply to experience the 1,000 or so pubs sprinkled liberally throughout the city (as the bridal and grooms parties do!).

Dublin is synonymous with pubs and for many tourists the first item on the 'to-do' list is to order a pint of Guinness. That particular beverage is found in almost every one of the glut of pubs dotted around the capital, but whether the establishment is as traditional as the drink is another question! Of course, the old–style porter houses still exist, but many are giving way to hip new joints designed with Scandinavian minimalism or Manhattan chic in mind. Arthur Guinness would turn in his grave!

It's not just the pubs that have changed. Dublin's (and Ireland's) traditional image as a parochial, insular place has undergone a reappraisal in recent years. You're more likely to be served balti than bacon, and with the likes of

Kilkenny Café

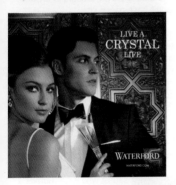

LIVE A
CRYSTAL
LIFE

WATERFORD
WATERFORD.COM

History
of Ireland

STERLING SILVER PENDANT
IRISH JEWELLERY CRAFTED FROM TRADITION

Kilkenny Shop & Café
Premium Fashion, Craft, Crystal & Food
in the Heart of Dublin

The iconic store & famous Kilkenny Cafe are situated
opposite the grounds of Trinity College on Nassau Street

Waterford Crystal, Gifts, Jewellery, Fashion & Accessories

Shipping Promotion Now On - Tax Free Shopping

6-15 Nassau Street, Dublin 2.

Chanel, Hermès, Louis Vuitton and Jimmy Choo opening their doors to the fashion–conscious of Dublin, it seems the city has decidedly entered into the international cosmopolitan arena.

And yet, for all this, there is clearly much more to Dublin than trendy bars and designer labels. Here is a city with a history and legacy that goes back over a thousand years, a history which has been as tumultuous and tragic as it has been heroic and triumphant. Then there are the city's people. Whether it exists in poverty or prosperity, Dublin's greatest asset has always been its inhabitants. Possessed of a wit and charm that is uniquely Irish, Dubliners are the beating heart of this vibrant, fast–paced city.

And it was these very inhabitants which James Joyce would immortalise in his masterpiece **Ulysses**, an epic charting a day in the life of Dubliner Leopold Bloom. This odyssey through the streets of Dublin, recounted entirely from memory, chronicles not only the make–up of a city but the mentality of a nation. It is this undeniable literary heritage which still defines much of Dublin's spirit and identity today.

Trinity College
One of Ireland's most renowned universities

One cannot wander through Dublin without taking into account its awesome literary past. This is the birthplace of the famously caustic playwright Oscar Wilde and of Nobel Prize winner Samuel Beckett. Jonathan Swift, the celebrated satirist who wrote **Gulliver's Travels** and whose statue stands outside Trinity College, was also a native of Dublin and the Sligo–born poet WB Yeats lived at 82 Merrion Square for a time. The list, like much of the banter in Dublin's pubs, is endless.

A mention of Merrion Square brings us neatly onto another topic close to many a Dubliner's heart:

Airfield; historic home, gardens, working farm and local food experience is just 20 minutes from the centre of Dublin.

farm café gardens home

Tel 01 969 6666   DUNDRUM   Co. DUBLIN   www.airfield.ie

its monuments and also architecture. One of Dublin's largest and most ornate squares, the architecture of Merrion Square is typical of the Georgian style seen in many of Dublin's buildings. Regarding monuments, whether it's the Molly Malone Statue on Grafton Street 'The Tart with the Cart' or the Millennium Spire on O'Connell Street 'The Stiletto in the Ghetto', Dublin's sculptures have always been a keen source of conversation and, at times, consternation!

Sunlight Chambers, Parliament Street

There has been an extremely successful campaign to renew eighteenth–century Georgian Dublin. A 'Golden Age' in the city's past, this period saw Dublin become one of Europe's most prepossessing capitals, graced with magnificent squares, elegant public buildings and long, wide streets. The Georgian aesthetic helped develop the beautiful Fitzwilliam and Merrion squares, as well as the James Gandon masterpiece, The Custom House, and imbued Dublin with much of the character it retains today. Added to this has been the city's commitment to urban renewal, visible in previously neglected areas such as the fashionable Temple Bar.

Dublin retains an edginess that makes the city such a fascinating contradiction. Nowhere is this more apparent than in Dublin's music scene. From fresh–faced buskers on Grafton Street to the traditional melodies that emanate from many of the pubs around the city, Dublin lives for music. If you want to listen to something a little more contemporary, venues such as the Olympia and Vicar Street offer good home–grown talent as well as exciting international artists.

Dublin, the 'dark pool', has something for everyone. Don't be fooled by the frothiness it has acquired in recent years. Dublin is too unique and multi–faceted to be reduced to a single stereotype and that, of course, is its ever–lasting charm.

COMMERCIAL FEATURE

NATIONAL MUSEUM OF IRELAND

National Museum of Ireland – Archaeology

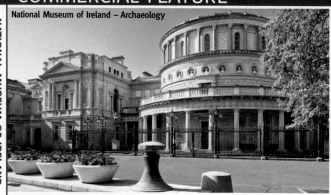

NATIONAL MUSEUM OF IRELAND

As Ireland's premier cultural institution, The National Museum of Ireland houses a vast array of collections which include objects of Irish material heritage, scientific specimen from the natural world as well as ancient artefacts from all over the globe.

Located at Collins Barracks, the Decorative Arts & History Museum houses an impressive thirteen permanent exhibitions in total. Among these, the museum examines the history of the Irish Military in the "Soldiers & Chiefs: The Irish at War at Home and Abroad since 1550" exhibition while also housing a large collection of silver, ceramics, glassware, costume and furniture, including works by the famous modern designer, Eileen Gray.

Housing over two million artefacts the Archaeology Museum's collection includes some of Ireland's most prized archaeological objects such as the Tara Brooch and the Ardagh Chalice. However, it is not only Irish treasures that lie within the depths of this 19th century building as exhibitions such as "Ancient Egypt" and "Life and Death in the Roman World" are also permanently on display.

An ecological haven in the heart of Dublin City the Natural History Museum exhibits not only species' of native Irish fauna such as badgers, deer, falcons and lobsters but also transforms into an exotic 'Dead Zoo' on the first floor housing creatures such as polar bears, kangaroos and tigers as well as suspending impressive whale skeletons from the museum roof.

Free admission to the greatest collections of Irish heritage, culture and history in the world.

Priceless treasures that belong to everyone

Family programmes & events for people of all ages.
For information visit:
www.museum.ie
Tel: 01 6777 444

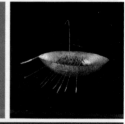

museum
National Museum of Ireland
Ard-Mhúsaem na hÉireann

Archaeology
Natural History
Decorative Arts & History
Country Life

Open:
Tuesday to Saturday
10am to 5pm.
Sunday 2pm to 5pm.
Closed:
Mondays including
Bank Holidays

TRAVEL TIPS & INFORMATION

Currency and Banking

The currency in Ireland is the **Euro** (€), which comes in notes of €500, €100, €50, €20, €10 and €5 and in coins of €1 and €2. Smaller denominations include the 50, 20, 10, 5, 2 and 1 cent coins. **Banks** are open between 10am and 4pm on Mondays, Tuesdays and Fridays, and stay open until 5pm on Thursdays. Some branches do not open until 10.30am on Wednesdays for staff training. **Bureau de Change** outlets tend to stay open **later.**

Transport

With a population of over 1 million, Dublin isn't a large city by world standards, but it is an extensive, low–rise one. The centre is compact and easily explored, but it's worth venturing further afield. To get around, you can travel by **DART** (Dublin Area Rapid Transit – the suburban rail line), by tram **(Luas)**, bus or by car.

The **DART (Dublin Area Rapid Transit)** is the rail line running along the coast of Dublin, from Malahide and Howth south–wards as far as Greystones, Co Wicklow. Weekly tickets are available at all ticket offices and also from the Travel

O'Connell Street

Centre, 35 Lower Abbey Street. Adult Rail, Adult Bus & Rail and Adult Luas & Rail are valid for one week's unlimited travel from date of purchase for 7 consecutive days.

The **Arrow** suburban railway network serves stations out to Dundalk, Arklow, Maynooth and Mullingar (all from Connolly station) and Kildare (from Heuston station). The Route 90 bus connects Connolly, Heuston and Tara Street stations.

Most buses run between 7am and 11.30pm and service all parts of the city. The **Nitelink**, a limited night service, operates on Thursdays, Fridays and Saturdays. You'll also find information about routes, schedules and tours at the **Dublin Bus Office** in O'Connell Street. If you don't pay the exact fare, you'll be given your change in the form of a receipt, which can only be redeemed at the Dublin Bus office. For this reason, it is often better to buy prepaid tickets at a newsagent.

Luas, Dublin's Tram System is a frequent, reliable and fast public transport option. There are two tram lines. The Luas Red Line runs from Tallaght or Saggart in the south west of Dublin to Connolly or The Point via Dublin's northern city centre.

The Luas Green Line runs from Brides Glen in south Dublin to St. Stephen's Green in the centre of Dublin's south city centre; services operate from Brides Glens or Sandyford to St. Stephen's Green. Trams operate from early morning to late evening with trams as frequent as every 3 minutes at peak and a maximum of up to 10–20 minutes frequency off peak. Tickets are available from ticket machines at each stop. See **www.luas.ie** for more information.

Aircoach provides a 24–hour luxury coach service between Dublin Airport and the city. They operate a number of routes, Ballsbridge and Leopardstown, which serve Dublin's top hotels and places of business and Cork. The service is ideally suited to tourists, commuters and the general public looking for a high-quality, reliable, clean and efficient service.

Car Rentals
If you're looking to rent a car, check out **Hertz**. You can pick up your hire car at the Hertz Desk in the Arrivals Hall at Dublin Airport or the Hertz Car Hire Office on South Circular Road. With Ireland's largest rental fleet, ranging from small city vehicles to larger family sized people carriers and a wide variety of automatic vehicles, Hertz has the car to meet your requirements.

Tours
Due to competition among operators, walking and bus tours in Dublin and also the surrounding region are very inexpensive and becoming ever more imaginative. The

number of 'themed' walking tours available in the city centre is phenomenal and they are a good way of getting your bearings.

Try the award–winning hop on hop off **Dublin City Sightseeing Tour**. The two day ticket comes with 28 stops, 2 routes and exclusive offers. Kids go free.

Dublin Bus runs open–top double-decker tours around the city throughout the year. Their Coast and Castle tours take you to the popular locations on the outskirts of the city, such as Malahide Castle and Howth. Check out the website located at **www.dublinbus.ie** for more details on tours.

Bus Éireann also provides day tours as well as a bus service that links Dublin city centre with cities and towns all around Ireland. Buses leave Dublin City Centre from Bus Áras, near The Custom House.

Extreme Ireland Tours offer quality and affordable day tours of Ireland for individuals and groups alike. They travel to some of the most popular destinations in Ireland, leaving every day from Dublin. They are one of the most flexible companies in the country with understanding and experienced guides who can cater for all your needs. Tours include: Cliffs Of Moher, Giant's Causeway, Belfast, Connemara, Cork & Blarney, the Celtic Boyne Valley Tour and The Gravedigger Ghost Tour.

Hilltoptreks provide a variety of guided walking tours throughout Ireland. Try the day tour from Dublin to Wicklow, Glendalough and enjoy hill walking, horse riding or mountain biking. Another popular tour is the Titanic, Belfast where you will visit The Titanic Centre and explore the Titanic story in a fresh, insightful way. They also offer novel walks such as Full Moon Walks and Photography Walks.

EXTREME IRELAND / IRISH DAY TOURS
College Green Tourism Office
37 College Green, Dublin 2
Tel: 00353-86-3169788
Email: info@daytours.ie
Web: www.daytours.ie

Our company offers quality and affordable DAY TOURS of Ireland for individuals and groups alike. Our destinations include; Cliffs Of Moher, Giant's Causeway, Belfast, Galway, Galway City, Connemara, Cork & Blarney, The Gravedigger and Folklore Tour and the Celtic Boyne Valley Tour.

HERTZ RENT A CAR
Hertz Dublin Airport,
Tel. 01 844 54 66
Hertz Downtown – South Circular Road,
Tel: 01 709 30 60
Hertz Downtown – Baggot St. Bridge,
Tel: 01 668 75 66
Email: Res@hertz.ie
Web: www.Hertz.ie

With cars available to suit all occasions and all rental lengths there is no better choice for car hire in Dublin. Fully insured and with the most competitive rates call us today at any of our Dublin branches. Hertz the #1 Car Rental Company in Dublin & Ireland.

HILLTOPTREKS
17 Dodder Lawn,
Dodder Valley Park,
Firhouse D24
Tel: +353 (0)87 7849 599
Email: Terry@Hilltoptreks.ie
Web: www.HilltopTreks.ie

At Hilltoptreks we offer guided walks and Tours. From 1 day tours with activity options to 8 day walking Holidays throughout Ireland. We also offer great novel walks such as our Full Moon Walks, and Photography Walks. We look after everything from the accommodation, luggage transfer and excellent guides for you. We can also facilitate private group outings and allow you to pick your itinerary for the tour.

IARNRÓD ÉIREANN
Connolly Station
Dublin 1
Tel: 1850 366 222
Email: info@irishrail.ie
Web: www.irishrail.ie

DART is one of the quickest ways to get you around Dublin.
Linking Dublin city via the scenic route of Dublin Bay, there are many interesting places along with historic towns and villages to picturesque harbours to enjoy along the way.

IRISH DAY TOURS

If you are looking to visit the best sights Ireland has to offer then take a tour with Irish Day Tours. Awarded a 5 star certificate of excellence by Tripadvisor last year, Irish Day Tours will ensure you take home some magical memories of your trip to Ireland. They offer a wide range of exciting guided coach tours visiting the most popular destinations in Ireland including the Cliffs of Moher, Giant's Causeway, Belfast, Connemara, Cork & Blarney Castle and some eerie night tours too!

Take an enchanting adventure with tour guides that are not only entertaining but their alluring accents will put a smile on your face. Visit one of Ireland's 7 wonders at the Cliffs of Moher on Wild West coast. This is the top attraction outside of Dublin and is a must see! Or visit one of the most northerly points of Ireland at the Giant's Causeway, recently listed as a World Heritage site. Explore the various stone formations and crevices that are fully engulfed with fascinating history as well as mysterious Irish folklore.

For those of you looking for some evening entertainment step on board the Traditional Irish Storytelling bus or the eerie Gravedigger Tour. This ghoulish 4D tour will remove you from reality, even if just for a little while!

So visit www.irishdaytours.ie or call 014100700 to make your booking today!

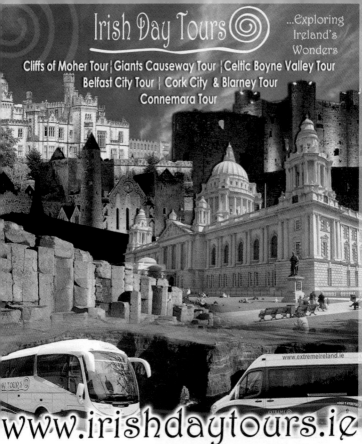

VISITOR'S GUIDE

South of the Liffey

If you're visiting Dublin for the first time and want to see as much of the city as possible, it's advisable to start your tour south of the River Liffey. It is possible to take in many of the city's attractions on foot and do not be dissuaded by the fast and furious pace of your fellow pedestrians. The main tourist attractions on the south side of the river are Trinity College, Temple Bar, Dublin Castle, The National Museums and Gallery, the National Concert Hall and the Guinness Storehouse.

If Ireland's cultural and historical past eludes you and it's shopping you're after, you might want to start off on the pedestrianised, red brick thoroughfare of **Grafton Street**. As one of Dublin's busiest and most lucrative shopping areas, its paving is lined with prestigious and long–standing businesses.

As you travel toward **College Green** you'll encounter the bronze statue of Molly Malone 'wheeling her barrow through streets broad and narrow'. On your right, secure behind high stone walls, is **Trinity College Dublin (TCD)**, which occupies forty acres of the city centre and is the city's most famous tourist attraction.

The Long Room,
Trinity College

Traditionally, Trinity was a Protestant university (founded by Queen Elizabeth I in 1592) and was then regarded by hidebound Catholics as a nest of dangerous ideas. As late as the 1960's, Catholics could not attend the college without a special dispensation and many tended to continue their education at **University College Dublin (UCD)**. The college is built around a series of cobbled quadrangles. Its best–known landmark is the thirty–metre

Campanile, which houses the university's bells and is
surrounded by venerable maple trees in Library Square.
The **Old Library** building holds Ireland's greatest treasure,
the **Book of Kells**. This illuminated copy of the Gospels,
written by monks around A.D. 800, is one of the oldest
books in the world. A decoratively illustrated work of
art, it is a masterpiece and testament to the labours of
its authors.

The Long Room, one of the oldest libraries in Ireland,
houses a collection of marble busts as well as Ireland's
earliest known harp, the Brian Ború harp, which dates
back to the fifteenth century. With its enormous vaulted
ceiling, the Long Room is home to 200,000 of Trinity's
oldest books and manuscripts. The student libraries in
Trinity – the Berkeley, the Lecky and its newest extension,
the Ussher – house an extensive collection of books that
Trinity, as a copyright library, receives.

Molly Malone statue
at the end of
Grafton Street

Bram Stoker, Jonathan Swift and
Oscar Wilde are among the great
Irish writers who graduated from
Trinity College. Samuel Beckett
was a former alumnus and later
spent a few miserable years
lecturing at the college. He drank
in the local pubs, and the famous
episode in his novel **More Pricks
than Kicks**, when the hero Belacqua
vomits over a policeman's boot
near the gates of Trinity College,
may well be biographical.

Moving opposite Trinity College
stands the classical **Bank of Ireland**, which was constructed
in 1729 as the seat of the Irish Parliament. The former
House of Commons has been absorbed into the bank,
while the oak–lined House of Lords has remained intact.
Its centrepiece is an 18th century chandelier made from
1,223 pieces of glass.

City Hall on Dame Street is an outstanding example of
the Georgian architecture for which Dublin is world–
renowned. Audioguides and leaflets are available in
different languages e.g. English, Irish, German, Spanish,
Italian and French. The building is fully wheelchair accessible.
The vaults now host the multi–media exhibition, 'Dublin's
City Hall: The Story of the Capital'. This exhibition traces
the evolution of Ireland's capital city, from before the
Anglo–Norman invasion of 1170 to the present day.

Behind the Bank of Ireland lies **Temple Bar**. Officially
described as 'Dublin's Cultural Quarter', Temple Bar is
bordered by Westmoreland Street, Dame Street, the
Quays and Parliament Street. Check out the innovative
modern architecture around **Meeting House Square**,
which also hosts an outdoor food market on Saturday
mornings and afternoons.

The National Wax Museum Plus is an exciting interactive visitor attraction located in the heart of Dublin's city centre Temple Bar district and just off Dame Street, designed to take you on a journey through Irish cultural heritage. If you are feeling brave, pay a visit to the Chambers of Horrors where Dracula and Hannibal Lector reside.

The Irish Museum of Modern Art is Ireland's leading national institution for the collection and presentation of modern and contemporary art. The museum is housed in the Royal Hospital Kilmainham, the finest 17th–century building in Ireland. The permanent Collection of the Irish Museum of Modern Art comprises some 1,650 works. Admission is free except for occasional special exhibitions.

Marked by dereliction and rejuvenation, **Temple Bar** was revitalised in the 1990's; now it is the artsy, suave

and expensive end of the city. Its cobbled enclaves are home to a host of trendy restaurants and pubs, eclectic galleries and shops. If **Temple Bar** is the heart of Dublin, it also connects spectacular and historically distinct areas: **Grafton Street** and **Trinity College** with **Christ Church Cathedral** and **Dublin Castle**.

The RHA Gallery (Royal Hibernian Academy), located just a 2 minute walk from St. Stephens Green, is one of Dublin's leading public art galleries. Open 7 days a week with free admission, the RHA gallery shows an innovative mix of Irish and International contemporary art. With an exhibition and education programme dedicated to developing, affirming and challenging the public's appreciation of traditional and innovative approaches to the visual arts, see www.rhagallery.ie to find out about their current exhibitions.

Viking Dublin extended over the area now bounded by **Dublin Castle** and Christ Church. Dublin was an important enough stronghold to merit mention in the Viking sagas.

Chester Beatty
Library

A portion of a Viking fortress is on view in the undercroft of Dublin Castle, which is situated on Dame Street in the heart of historic Dublin. The city gets its name from 'Dubh Linn' (black pool), an area thought to be roughly where the Castle Garden is today. The south range of the Castle complex houses the State Apartments, which were once the residential quarters of the Vice Regal Court.

Dublinia & The Viking World is a heritage centre, located in central Dublin, at the heart of the medieval city. The exhibitions at Dublinia explore life in the medieval city and the world of the Vikings and contain life–sized reconstructions which will take you back to Viking and Medieval Dublin with a variety of sights, sounds, and smells. Housed in a beautiful neo– Gothic Victorian building, the former Synod Hall of the Church of Ireland, this landmark building was acquired in the late 1980's by parent body, The Medieval Trust. The Trust has worked to preserve this building as part of their ongoing work.

Another Viking must–see attraction are the **Viking Splash Tours**, which take you on a fun tour of Viking Dublin by land and water by travelling on board the vintage, amphibious, military World War 11 vehicles called "Ducks". Tours depart from Stephens Green North close to Grafton Street and are suitable for the whole family.

One of the highlights of a trip to Dublin Castle is the **Chester Beatty Library**. Sir Alfred Chester Beatty was an American mining magnate and a discerning and idiosyncratic collector of the religious treasures he encountered during his sixty years of travelling in Europe and the Far East. The collection is now commanding the attention it deserves, having been moved from a suburban house in Ballsbridge to the Clock Tower building at Dublin Castle in 1999.

Christ Church Cathedral predates Dublin Castle by a century, making it Dublin's oldest building. The original cathedral was built by the Viking king **Sitric Silkenbeard**. In 1169, the Norman Earl of Pembroke, **Richard de Clare** (Strongbow), ordered the present building to be built after his conquest of the city. He was not to live to see its completion. After many restorations the cathedral is a hybrid of architectural styles.

To the south of Christ Church Cathedral lies **Saint Patrick's Cathedral.** Founded in 1191, it is best–known for its association with the writer and satirist **Jonathan**

Saint Patrick's Cathedral

Saint Patrick's Cathedral, Dublin
Open Daily for Visitors

www.stpatrickscathedral.ie
Tel: 00353 1 4539472

National Gallery of Ireland

Swift who was Dean there from 1713 to 1745. The combined choirs of St Patrick's and Christ Church first performed **Handel's Messiah** here in 1742. Built in honour of Ireland's patron saint, **Saint Patrick's Cathedral** stands adjacent to the famous well where tradition has it Saint Patrick baptized converts on his visit to Dublin. The Cathedral is open to everyone as an architectural and historical site.

To appreciate more of Ireland's past, the **National Museum of Archaeology** and History can be found on Kildare Street. The museum's holdings represent the entire sweep of Irish history, from the Stone Age to the present day. One such display, **Ireland's Gold**, is one of the finest collections of prehistoric, gold artefacts in Europe. The main exhibit is the exquisite Broighter boat, a gold vessel complete with oars, mast and spar found by a farmer a hundred years ago on the shores of Lough Foyle. **The Treasury,** is the museum's key attraction, contains outstanding examples of Celtic and Medieval art, such as the Ardagh Chalice, the Tara Brooch and the Derrynaflan Hoard – a definite must–see.

The National Gallery of Ireland was founded by an Act of Parliament in 1854 and opened to the public in 1864. Today it houses some 13,000 works comprising the national collection of Irish and European fine art. Highlights of the Irish collection include works by James Barry, Nathaniel Hone I, Hugh Douglas Hamilton, Thomas Roberts, William Orpen, John Lavery, Roderic O'Conor, Paul Henry, Mainie Jellett, Louis le Brocquy and Gerard Dillon.

Fine Art Photographic Prints by
Irish Photographer John Barrett

Prints can be viewed and purchased upon request at
www.saatchionline.com/Johnbarrett

Also on Merrion Street is the **National Museum of Ireland's Natural History Museum**. This oldest part of the museum, which has been open for more than 150 years, houses a fine collection of both native and foreign fauna. A visit to the **Natural History Museum** is an excellent way to keep children (and adults) amused on a rainy Dublin afternoon.

Situated between two national institutes, the **National Library** and National Museum, **Leinster House** on Kildare Street, has been the seat of the Oireachtas, or Irish Parliament, since 1925. Completed in 1748, it was the first great eighteenth century house to be built south of the Liffey, and

St Patrick's Cathedral

has been claimed as the prototype for the White House in the United States. Much of what you see around you in central Dublin dates back to the prosperous Georgian era of the eighteenth and late nineteenth centuries.

During the eighteenth century, as the city grew rapidly in size and population, the medieval walls were swept away and new broad streets and elegant squares were

Dublin Castle

built on reclaimed land on either side of the Liffey. From the 1750's onwards, great town houses were erected around Fitzwilliam Square and Merrion Square, the centre of which was laid out as a public park. In the restored **Newman House** on St Stephen's Green, which joins two fine Georgian buildings, you'll see magnificent eighteenth century interiors and beautiful plaster decoration.

If it's culture of the musical variety that takes your fancy, the **National Concert Hall** on Earlsfort Terrace, just off St Stephen's Green, often holds lunchtime concerts.

Close by at 33 Synge Street, **The Shaw Birthplace** is a real gem. This Victorian home mirrors the early life of the renowned Irish playwright, George Bernard Shaw.

St Stephen's Green is Ireland's best– known Victorian city park. It covers nine hectares of the city centre and is at its best in the summer when the tree–lined walks, flowerbeds and ornamental lakes provide colourful relief from the hustle and bustle of the streets. The park is littered with statues that commemorate some of Ireland's literary and political heroes, like Robert Emmet, James Joyce, Countess Markiewitz and W.B. Yeats.

Once a common ground for grazing animals, it was transformed into a park in 1887, with the helpful funding of **Sir Arthur Edward Guinness**, later to be known as Lord Ardilaun. A statue dedicated to the latter stands with its head directed toward **St James's Gate**, where he was the proprietor of the family business, the Guinness brewery. No self–appraising tourist could come to Dublin without

Guinness
Storehouse

stopping off at the **Guinness Storehouse**. Chances are you'll smell the place before you see it as the prevailing westerly winds carry the tang of roasting barley across the city. Located at the heart of the St. James's Gate brewery, **Guinness Storehouse** is Ireland's No.1 International visitor attraction.

From the Guinness Storehouse on Thomas Street to Inchicore to Military Road you can take in the finest sights to be seen south of the Liffey.

Forbidding **Kilmainham Gaol** on Inchicore Road is the largest unoccupied prison in the British Isles and was a place of punishment and execution for criminals and Nationalists between 1796 and 1924 when it closed. It's certainly recommended to anyone with an interest in Irish history.

Of equal historical merit is the magnificent seventeenth century **Royal Hospital Building** on Military Road, which now houses **The Irish Museum of Modern Art** (IMMA), Ireland's leading institution for the preservation and collection of modern and contemporary art. Its spacious grounds include a formal garden, meadows and medieval burial grounds.

The Four Courts

North of the Liffey

The Liffey is a useful reference point when trying to find your bearings in Dublin. If you're in a walking mood, follow the north quays of the Liffey from town, past the **Four Courts** and **Smithfield** right up to the entrance of the Phoenix Park on Parkgate Street. Alternatively, take the number 90 bus from Aston Quay to Heuston Station; these attractions are on the other side of the river.

The National Museum of Ireland at **Collin's Barracks** is located along this walking route and houses the Museum of Decorative Arts and History. It is our country's premier cultural institution and home to the greatest collections of Irish material heritage, culture and natural history in the world. With a frequently changing programme of exhibitions, as well as fabulous exhibitions of coins, furniture, costume and clothing, it is a great way to break up the walk to the Park.

Hanging barrel at Jameson Distillery

The Park extends over 1,750 acres and it feels at times as if you're in open countryside. Deer, introduced during colonial times, roam freely. In case you and yours get separated, arrange to rendezvous at the **Papal Cross**, which was erected in 1979 for the visit of Pope John Paul II to Ireland.

Áras an Uachtaráin is the residency of Ireland's president and can be located by the beautiful **Phoenix**

Column. The house was once the residence of the British Lord Lieutenant. In an infamous incident, two British officials were stabbed to death close to this area in 1882, one of the many violent episodes which led up to the 1916 Rising.

The fully restored **Ashtown Castle** in Phoenix Park is a medieval tower house that probably dates from the 17th century. There is also a restaurant in the grounds of the Visitor Centre. A lively and entertaining exhibition on the history and wildlife of the Park is on display in the Visitor Centre.

Dublin Zoo is one of Ireland's top visitor attractions and is located in the Phoenix Park. There's something for everyone at this spectacular Zoo. Look out for keeper talks and animal feeding times. Animals here include giraffes, zebras, Asian elephants, tigers, hippos, red pandas and orangutans to name only a few. Dine at the unique Meerkat Restaurant where you can look out for these inquisitive animals as you enjoy your meal.

Smithfield is at the centre of one of the most imaginative civic restoration projects undertaken in Dublin. Gas–lamps arranged around the square look like giant birds poised for flight. The Lighthouse Cinema offers a unique cultural aspect to the area, while the **Old Jameson Distillery** remains the largest footfall attraction. Hop on the Luas which will take you to The National Museum, the Old Jameson Distillery and to the bustling shopping area at Jervis.

Take a trip through the romantic past of Irish whiskey making at **The Old Jameson Distillery** in Smithfield, one of Dublin's top visitor attractions. Set in the heart of historic Dublin, the Old Jameson Distillery dates back to 1780 with the visitor centre being housed within the original four walls where John Jameson founded the distillery. Rich in history, the centre provides a wonderful insight into the fine art of whiskey making with an audio visual presentation, a walk through the recreated distillery and a whiskey tasting in the **Jameson Discovery Bar** where you can enjoy a complimentary glass of Jameson and a

The Ilac Centre

TK·MAXX

H&M

DEBENHAMS   DUNNES STORES   RIVER ISLAND

80 stores | 13 eateries | 1,000 car parking spaces from only €2 per hour

● Fashion ● Gifts ● Jewellery ● Footwear ● Homewares ●
● Sportswear ● Accessories ● Hairdressing ●
● Toys ● Health Products ● Newsagents ● Library ●
● Tranquility Room ● Internet

www.ilac.ie

O'Connell Street & The GPO

chance to become a "Qualified Irish Whiskey Taster". Linger a little longer in the plush Reserve Bar with a Jameson Irish Coffee or simply browse the Distillery Gift Shop for a special memento of your visit.

Having won the title of, "Best Venue for Dinner & Entertainment in all Ireland", three years in a row, the distillery boasts a range of entertainment facilities including **The 3rd Still Restaurant**, JJ's Bar and the popular Irish **'Shindig Nights'** of traditional Irish music, song and dance. Evening packages are available encompassing a guided tour, whiskey tasting, a four course meal and live Irish music and dancing. With over 200,000 visitors passing through the doors each year this is one experience not to be missed.

Moving down along the quays of the River Liffey, the influence of **James Gandon**, who is one of the greatest architects associated with the city, becomes apparent. Gandon designed **King's Inn** (1785) on Henrietta Street and the Four Courts (1802). All of these monuments date back to a period when Britain had briefly acknowledged the legislative independence of the Irish parliament. A brass plaque in **Drumcondra Churchyard** commemorates James Gandon (1742–1824).

The history of the **Four Courts** plays itself out in its occupation by the Nationalist anti–Treaty forces as part of their military headquarters. The Irish Civil War began when Michael Collins' pro–Treaty Free State army opened fire on the building on 28th June 1922, quickly reducing it to a blazing husk. During the attacks, vast amounts of valuable historical documents and records went up in smoke. The buildings have been overtime painstakingly restored, but the records of Irish history they once contained are long since gone.

O'Connell Street, the grandest boulevard in the city, had turned somewhat tatty over the last few decades but has recently undergone rapid restoration. And the most

James Joyce
Copper Statue,
North Earl Street

conspicuous and tallest structure in the city, Ian Ritchie's stainless steel **Dublin Spire**, was erected in the centre of O'Connell Street in January 2003 as a very belated replacement for **Nelson's Pillar**, which was a beloved Dublin landmark blown up by the Irish Republican Army (IRA) in 1966. Make what you will of this soaring steel needle; for some it is flimsy and alien, for others it is a monument of pure, abstract power. The Spire is visible from many points outside the city. It looks best at night when the perforated top section, lit by small LEDs, casts a ghostly grey–blue satin sheen.

The **GPO** (General Post Office) is remembered for much more than just delivering mail throughout the country. It marks the seminal moment in 20th–century Irish history when the Nationalist leader, **Padraig Pearse**, proclaimed Ireland a Republic on its steps on Easter Monday 1916. As he spoke, his heavily armed supporters were occupying and also reinforcing strategic positions around the city. The British finally dislodged them and forced their surrender after four days of bloody fighting which left hundreds dead and injured and much of the city centre in ruins. The secret executions of the leaders of the rising would later serve to increase and harden support for separatism in Ireland.

Visit **An Post Museum at the GPO**. This little museum looks at the remarkable influence of the Post Office on Irish life and society over the generations. Housed in Dublin's GPO, a beautiful building in its own right and headquarters of course of the 1916 rebels, it tells – through traditional display and clever interactive media – the fascinating story of Letters, Lives & Liberty.

While on O'Connell Street, look out for the famous **Clery's Department Store**. Lovers and friends alike have been 'meeting under Clery's clock', a famous Dublin landmark, for many years. The elegant **Gresham Hotel** is also a renowned meeting place on this famous old street.

The Ilac Centre opened in 1981 and was the first shopping centre in Dublin's city centre. The centre has undergone a €60m refurbishment in recent years and has been transformed into a bright and airy shopping venue all on one floor. The centre is home to the Central Library on the first floor with a small chapel underneath.

The former **St. Mary's Church of Ireland** is one of the earliest examples of a galleried church in Dublin. Built at the beginning of the 18th century, it boasts many outstanding features, such as the **Renatus Harris** built organ & spectacular stained glass window. The tasteful conversion and also refurbishment of this Dublin landmark was acknowledged at the Dublin City Neighbourhood Awards 2006, where it won first prize in the category of Best Old Building.

Important historical figures associated with St. Mary's include: **Arthur Guinness** – Founder of Guinness Brewery was married here in 1761, **Sean O'Casey** – Playwright & Author of "The Plough & The Stars", "Juno & The Paycock" & "The Shadow of a Gunman" was baptised here in 1880. **Theobald Wolf Tone** – United Irishmen Founder

was baptised here in 1763. Also, **John Wesley** – Founder of the Methodist Church delivered his first Irish sermon here in 1747. **Jonathan Swift** – Author of Gulliver's Travels and Dean of St. Patrick's Cathedral attended services here as did The Earl of Charlemont an Irish Volunteer.

George Frederic Handel's "Messiah" was first publicly performed in Dublin in April 1742 on Fishamble Street, and it is known that he regularly used the organ here to practice. Also, buried within the grounds are **Mary Mercer** – Founder of Mercer's Hospital and **Lord Norbury,** The Hanging Judge who ordered the execution of **Robert Emmett** in 1803.

Built by Daithi Hanly, **The Garden of Remembrance** can be found in the heart of the city and is dedicated to all those who lost their lives in the cause of Irish freedom. In 2011, the Queen laid a wreath there. The **1916 Moore Street Monument** was designated in 2007. It was on Moore Street that Irish Volunteers surrendered to British Forces during the Irish War of Independence.

The Ambassador Theatre is one of the city's most well-known venues, hosting many productions over the years including cinema, concerts and theatre. Another landmark theatre is **The Gate Theatre**, which offers high quality performances in a historic venue.

The Rotunda Hospital was founded in 1745 and moved to a new location in 1757. It was the first maternity hospital in Britain and Ireland and included a garden and concert hall. The Ambassador and Gate Theatres are part of this building.

Moving off O'Connell Street into **North Great George's Street**, you'll find the **James Joyce Cultural Centre**. No. 35 is an archive of portraits, photographs, books and tapes of Joyce. **Bloomsday** celebrates the great writer and **Ulysses** on June 16th every year, and the date had a particular significance for James Joyce as on that day in 1904 he and his girlfriend Nora Barnacle enjoyed their first act of intimacy.

Ulysses is set on this one day and charts the thoughts and reveries of two Dubliners, Leopold Bloom (a Jewish advertising clerk) and Stephen Daedalus (a young writer who was bitterly estranged from his father), as they wander through the city. To say that the novel was unfavourably received when it was first published in Paris back in 1922 would be an understatement: some critics found the loose experimental structure was unintelligible while others were revolted by the references to sex, adultery and bodily functions.

The English–speaking world would take a long time to embrace the novel. The US customs confiscated copies and British customs burned the book upon its arrival at the docks in Folkestone. The Irish authorities blacklisted it and **Ulysses** would not go on public sale in Dublin until the late 1960's. A few smuggled copies did circulate clandestinely among Ireland's writers, three of whom – **Anthony Cronin, Patrick Kavanagh, & Flann O'Brien** – celebrated the first Bloomsday on 16 June 1954 with a pub-crawl which started at the **Martello Tower** in Sandycove, where the first chapter of Ulysses takes place.

Today the tower is home to **The James Joyce Museum** which is devoted to the life and works of the acclaimed writer. **Bloomsday** (the centenary of which was celebrated in 2004 with numerous commemorative events) has become a renowned Dublin institution, with Joyce fans flocking to the city from all over the world.

The Dublin City Gallery, The Hugh Lane is housed in the grand eighteenth–century **Charlemont House** on **Parnell Square** and has the largest public collection of 20th century Irish art, as well as works by contemporary Irish and foreign artists. Its holdings include Impressionist masterpieces by Renoir, Degas, Monet and Berth Morisot.

A recent acquisition is the **Francis Bacon Studio,** which was moved, contents and all, from the late artist's home in Reece Mews in London to the Gallery. A few doors up, also on Parnell Square, is the **Dublin Writers Museum**. Housed in a magnificent 18th century mansion, this museum is a celebration of Ireland's literary tradition and its many talented writers.

The Custom House, one of the most stunning and also commanding buildings on the north bank of the Liffey, is a telling example of history, warfare and restitution. Originally designed by James Gandon in 1781, the Custom House, the seat of the nine administrative departments, was destroyed by a five day fire during the greatest urban operation of the War of Independence. Fortunately, it was rebuilt according to its original design.

The Dublin Docklands Area is the focus of the new developments in the city. At the west end of the Docklands stands the highly successful and the impressively designed **International Financial Services Centre (IFSC)**. In recent years, **The Docklands' Walking Trail** has been launched and trail maps and information are available from the Dublin Docklands offices and at Dublin Tourism.

The Croke Park Experience is a must–see for anyone interested in the history and development of Ireland's national games of **hurling** and **Gaelic football**. Go behind the scenes with this fantastic tour that offers an in–depth look at one of the most historic and modern sporting arenas in the world. Don't miss the **Etihad Skyline**, Croke Park roof-top tour and the panoramic views of the city.

The **Glasnevin Museum** which opened in recent years on the Finglas Road is another must–see Dublin attraction for anyone interested in Irish Heritage & Genealogy. The exhibitions on view seek to show the social, historical, political and artistic development of modern Ireland through the lives of the generations buried in Ireland's Necropolis. Glasnevin Trust offers walking tours led by Historian Shane MacThomais.

The Casino, located at Marino, Dublin 3 was designed by Sir William Chambers as a pleasure house for James Caulfield, 1st Earl of Charlemont and is one of the finest 18th century neo–classical buildings in Europe. Access is by guided tour only.

UNMISSABLE

CROKE PARK. THE TRUE IRISH EXPERIENCE.

One of Ireland's Top Tourist Attractions.

Follow in the footsteps of legends on a stadium tour

Take in the best views of Dublin from the roof of Croke Park

Enjoy an interactive visitor experience at the GAA Museum

CROKE PARK *Experience*

ETIHAD SKYLINE CROKE PARK STADIUM

GAA MUSEUM CROKE PARK

crokepark.ie

Bus Stop 24a

AN POST MUSEUM GPO, O'Connell Street, Dublin 1 Tel: 01 7057000 Email: heritage@anpost.ie Web: www.anpost.ie/heritage	From stamps and mail boats to the role of GPO staff on Easter Monday 1916 **Letters, Lives and Liberty** at the An Post Museum tells the story of how the Post Office has played a vital role in the development of Irish society over the generations.
AIRFIELD Overend Way Dundrum, Dublin 14 Tel: 01 9696666 Email: info@airfield.ie Web: www.airfield.ie	Welcome to Airfield, an historic home, food & ornamental gardens, 38 acre working farm and a local food experience, all only 20 minutes from the centre of Dublin on the Luas. Join us for a day of fascinating history, gorgeous food, farm animals, woodland walks and nature at her finest.
CITY HALL Dame Street, Dublin 2 Tel: +353 1 222 2204 Fax: +353 1 222 2620 Email: cityhall@dublincity.ie Web: www.dublincity.ie	Welcome to Dublin's City Hall, the headquarters of Dublin City Council. Originally built as a Royal Exchange, the vaults of City Hall now host a multi-media exhibition The Story of the Capital which traces the evolution of Ireland's capital city, from before the Anglo-Norman invasion of 1170 to the present day.
CHESTER BEATTY LIBRARY Dublin Castle, Dublin 2 Tel: +353 1 4070750 Fax: +353 1 4070760 Email: info@cbl.ie Web: www.cbl.ie	World–renowned art museum & library, with unique exhibitions of manuscripts, prints, rare books, drawings and decorative arts from countries across Asia, the Middle East, North Africa and Europe. Admission FREE.
CROKE PARK STADIUM TOURS, GAA MUSEUM & ETIHAD SKYLINE Cusack Stand, St. Joseph's Avenue, Croke Park, Dublin 3 Phone: +353 (0)1 819 2323 Fax: +353 (0)1 819 2324 Email: gaamuseum@crokepark.ie Email: skyline@crokepark.ie. Website: crokepark.ie/gaa-museum Website: skylinecrokepark.ie	Behind the scenes guided tour at one of Ireland's top visitor attractions and most iconic sporting arenas full of sporting and cultural heritage. GAA Museum offers an interactive visitor experience and the Etihad Skyline gives visitors a panoramic view of Dublin from the roof top tour. Top 5 ranked Dublin visitor attraction on TripAdvisor!
DUBLINIA St. Michaels Hill, Christchurch, Dublin 8 Tel: 01-6794611 Mail: info@dublinia.ie Web: www.dublinia.ie	Dublinia, open 10-6.30 (March to September) and 10-5.30 (October to February). Dublinia is one of Dublin's top attractions with three exciting exhibitions, located at the historic crossroads of old Dublin. Viking and Medieval Dublin bring the city to life in an exciting way for all ages to learn and share. Also unearth the city's past at the History Hunters exhibition.

GUINNESS STOREHOUSE
St. James's Gate,
Dublin 8
Tel: +353 1 408 4800
Fax: +353 1 408 4965
Email guinness-storehouse@guinness.com
Web: www.guinness-storehouse.com

Located in the heart of the St. James's Gate Brewery, Guinness Storehouse is a seven-storey visitor experience dedicated to the history and making of this world famous beer. Book online at www.guinness-storehouse.com to skip the queue and receive a 10% discount off adult tickets.

NATIONAL MUSEUM OF IRELAND – ARCHAEOLOGY, KILDARE ST, D2

NATIONAL MUSEUM OF IRELAND – NATURAL HISTORY, MERRION ST, D2

NATIONAL MUSEUM OF IRELAND – DECORATIVE ARTS & HISTORY, COLLINS BARRACKS, D7
Phone: 01 6777444
Fax: 01 6777450
Email: marketing@museum.ie

Web: www.museum.ie
Follow us on Facebook and Twitter.

The National Museum of Ireland - Archaeology, Kildare Street, Dublin 2. Natural History, Merrion Street, Dublin 2 and Decorative Arts & History, Collins Barracks, Dublin 7. Opening hours: Tuesday-Saturday 10am-5pm, Sunday 2pm-5pm. Closed Mondays (incl. Bank Holidays). Admission Free.

RHA GALLERY,
Royal Hibernian Academy,
15 Ely Place, Dublin 2
Tel: +353 (0)1 661 2558
Email: info@rhagallery.ie
Web: www.rhagallery.ie

Located just 3 minutes walk from St. Stephens Green, Dublin's RHA Gallery is one of Irelands leading arts organisations with a proud history of promoting the visual arts in Ireland, open seven days a week, with free admission.

SAINT PATRICK'S CATHEDRAL
Saint Patrick's Close,
Dublin 8
Tel: 00353 1 4539472
Email: tours@stpatrickscathedral.ie
Web: www.stpatrickscathedral.ie

Founded in 1191, Jonathan Swift was Dean from 1713-1745. Music plays an integral part in the daily life in the Cathedral and the building is open to all people as both an architectural and historical site, but principally as a place of worship.

OLD JAMESON DISTILLERY
Bow Street,
Smithfield,
Dublin 7
Tel: +353 (0) 1 8072348
Fax: +353 (0) 1 8072369
Email: ojd@jamesonwhiskey.com
Web: www.jamesonwhiskey.com/tours

Visit the Old Jameson Distillery where our expert guides will lead you, from grain to glass, through the fascinating story of Jameson Irish Whiskey.

Offering Guided Tours 7 days a week, Tutored Whiskey Tasting, Exclusive Gift Shop, Restaurant & Bars.

Ireland's ever growing population and Dublin's magnetic appeal has meant that the capital has developed into a sprawling metropolis, rivalling Europe's major cities.

South County Dublin

The Southside has a great deal of attractions. **Blackrock** (on the DART line) offers excellent shopping and bargain prices at its weekend market, and also swanky boutiques and lively pubs. **Dun Laoghaire** (also on the DART line) is a seaside suburb and the ferry gateway to the UK. One of its main features is its expansive harbour, marked by its East and West piers, each of which is punctuated with lighthouses. Dun Laoghaire also has a range of glass–fronted restaurants offering excellent views over the pier and out to sea.

Within walking distance of Dun Laoghaire is **Sandycove**, famous for its circular **Martello Towers**, which were part of a coastal defence system created by the British during the Napoleonic Wars. The tower at Sandycove was the residence of **Oliver St John Gogarty** in 1904, and it was here he invited his young friend James Joyce to stay with him.

Little has changed since 1904; the gun platform, with its views over Dublin Bay and the living room inside the tower are much as they were in Joyce's day. Some of his letters and possessions are on display here, alongside rare and first editions of some of his works. **Silvia Beach,** the first publisher of Ulysses, opened the **Joyce Museum** in 1962. The Edwardian main street of

Swimming at the Forty Foot

the adjoining village of **Glasthule** is an interesting mix of trendy cafés and pubs and shops selling designer labels, antiques, fine foods and much more.

The nearby **Forty Foot** was once a popular spot for male-only nude bathing. Today, skinny–dipping is now discouraged and some brave women can also be seen taking the icy plunge into the Irish Sea.

Further down the south coast, and only thirty minutes from the city centre by DART, **Dalkey** is an affluent residential area and a popular location for weekend excursions. You can work up an appetite for a visit to one of the many restaurants in the quaint village with a stroll down **Coliemore Road** to **Bullock Harbour** where you can take a boat out over Joyce's 'snot–green sea' to **Lambay Island**.

A walk up to the obelisk on top of **Killiney Hill** is a great way to work off any over-indulgence in Dalkey Village and the views are well worth the effort!

Airfield Farm & Gardens in Dundrum is Dublin's only 38 acre working farm that is open to the public. It is a charitable organisation established by the Overend family in 1974 for educational and recreational purposes. Perfect for a family day out, experience the animals on the farm including the milking Jersey herd, sheep, donkeys and hens. Explore the gardens at your own pace or opt for a heritage tour of the Overend family home.

Rathfarnham Castle in Dublin 14 was built by Adam Loftus, an ambitious Yorkshire clergyman who rose to become Archbishop of Dublin, Lord Chancellor of Ireland and was involved in the establishment of Trinity College. Visitors can view the fine 18th century interiors by Sir William Chambers and James 'Athenian' Stuart.

The Pearse Museum in the beautiful St Enda's Park, Dublin 16 was a former school run by Patrick Pearse.

Attractions include exhibitions, a nature study room with attractive displays on Irish flora and fauna and an audio visual show entitled "This Man Kept a School."

North County Dublin

If you follow your compass arrow and head to Dublin's northern suburbs, you'll find yourself in **Fingal**, comprising the northern area of old County Dublin. Among a number of suburb towns that stand out are **Castleknock** – where Hollywood hotshot Colin Farrell was born and reared and next door **Blanchardstown**, which has a large and expanding shopping centre.

If shopping isn't on your agenda, the fishing town of **Howth**, with its piers and marina on the seaward side of the peninsula, is a popular destination for Dubliners at weekends. Howth was once an island, but is now linked to the mainland by the prosperous, low–lying suburb of **Sutton**.

For a bracing walk and fantastic views, follow the signs for Howth summit. Once there, you'll see the **Bailey Lighthouse** on its jutting outcrop of rock below you. Beyond it is the sweep of Dublin Bay, and further away

Malahide Castle

LISTINGS

MALAHIDE CASTLE & GARDENS
Malahide
Co. Dublin
Tel: +353 1 8169538
Email: reservations@shannonheritage.com
Web: www.malahidecastleandgardens.ie

Malahide Castle & Gardens are a must see on any visit to Dublin. Located on Dublin's beautiful north coast just 13km from Dublin City centre, Malahide Castle is one of Ireland's oldest castles, dating back to the 12th century. Daily guided tours from 9.30am. Open all year round.

still the Wicklow Mountains. And if you're feeling really energetic, walk or cycle along the northern shore of Dublin Bay between **Clontarf** and Sutton on to **Bull Island**, a man–made island built by Captain William Bligh (of Mutiny on the Bounty fame).

Visit the historic landmark that is **Malahide Castle and Gardens**, one of the oldest castles in Ireland. Enjoy a guided tour that will take you on a journey through the history of the Talbot Family and the legacy they left behind. The ornamental gardens adjoining the castle cover an area of about 22 acres. Over 5000 difference species and varieties of plants are present.

Other Northside attractions which are vying for attention are **Portmarnock** and **Malahide**. Both the villages are famous for their beaches, but there are many other outstanding beaches in Fingal, including **Skerries**, **Donabate**, and **Portrane**, where the sea is very shallow and the sands are rarely crowded, even on the sunniest day.

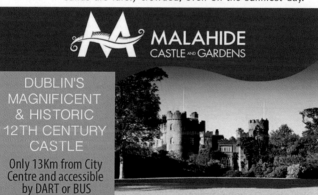

OUTSIDE DUBLIN

If you fancy extending your travels, there are also many attractions located within a one or two hour drive of the capital which are there to be enjoyed.

County Kildare

Kildare, the rich farming county to the west of Dublin, is the centre of Ireland's famous horse–breeding industry and is also an excellent golfing county. **The National Stud**, established by Colonel Hall Walker in 1945 to improve the quality of the national bloodstock, has been significant in establishing Ireland as a major player in world racing.

For a spiritual lift, visit the **Japanese Gardens**. These were laid out by Tassa Eida and his son between 1906 and 1910. Intending the garden to symbolise the soul's journey from oblivion to eternity, the Eidas planted oriental trees and shrubs along what they called 'paths of beauty'.

Castletown House in County Kildare is Ireland's largest and earliest Palladian style house. It was built between 1722 and 1729 for William Conolly, Speaker of the Irish House of Commons and the wealthiest commoner in Ireland. Take a tour and learn about the history of this house and view the fine architecture, original furniture and vast collection of paintings within Castletown.

If shopping grabs your interest a visit to **Kildare Village Outlet** shopping is advised. This is the ultimate shopping destination only sixty minutes from Dublin and features fabulous, year–round reductions on over 40 sought–

Castletown House after designer brands specialising in wardrobe and home luxuries, beauty products and premium accessories. Kildare Village has become a hot spot since its July 2006 opening with an unrivalled shopping experience offering unbeatable bargains on sought – after designer brands within an attractive village ambience.

CASTLETOWN

House, Parklands, Courtyard Café, Events & Conference Centre

An Italian Palazzo by the River Liffey

FREE admission to the restored 18th century designed landscape, open daily.

House and Café open daily from 14th March to 31st October 2015.

Private groups/School tours available throughout the year upon prior arrangement.

Axel Bernstorff

www.castletown.ie

castletown@opw.ie
Castletown House, Celbridge, Co. Kildare
Tel: +353 1 628 8252
Facebook: Castletown House & Parklands
Facebook: Heritage Ireland
Twitter: @opwcastletown

20km from Dublin City Centre
Free parking: Exit 6, M4, Celbridge West
Dublin Bus: 67 from Merrion Square to Main Street Celbridge

County Meath

County Meath is central to the history of Ireland and among its most popular tourist locations are the Neolithic site of **Newgrange** in the Boyne Valley and the **Hill of Tara**. From these sites the views of the surrounding countryside are spectacular. **Brú na Bóinne** is a world heritage site, dominated by the three well–known 5,000 year old large passage tombs: Knowth, Newgrange and Dowth. Newgrange is open all year round while Knowth is open from April to October. At the visitor centre, the exhibition takes approximately one hour, but the exhibition and Newgrange takes two hours. Note you can only access Newgrange and Knowth through a guided tour beginning at the the the **Brú na Bóinne Visitor Centre**.

Nearby is **Slane Castle**, home of the Earl of Mount Charles. Capability Brown planned the gardens and park, which are these days best–known as a venue for large open air rock music concerts.

The **Battle of the Boyne** started on the Louth (north) bank when the forces of King William ('King Billy') crossed the river to outflank those of the ousted Catholic King James II. The battle ranged across the Oldbridge Estate on the Meath (south) bank, where there is now a display of replica weaponry and recreations of army life in the seventeenth century.

Also in Meath you will find **Trim Castle** in Trim Town Centre. Trim is a heritage town. It is the largest Anglo-Norman castle in the country, built over a thirty year period by Hugh de Lacy and his son Walter. The castle was built on the site of an earlier wooden fortress, burned down by the Irish during British rule. Take a guided tour and walk around the grounds and keep.

County Wicklow

County Wicklow is nicknamed the 'Garden of Ireland' because of its lush and mountainous landscape and its

picturesque villages and small towns. A must see is **Glendalough** (the Valley of the Two Lakes), an ancient monastic site located in a deep, glacial valley high up in the Wicklow Mountains. The valley of the two lakes has long been a draw to people from all over the country and beyond thanks to the area's stunning scenery and rich heritage. At the **Glendalough Visitor Centre**, discover the history of this early Christian ecclesiastical settlement founded by St. Kevin in the 6th century through the exhibition and audio-visual show. Guided tours are available on request.

County Offaly

While in Offaly, make sure to drop in to the **Tullamore Dew Visitor Centre**. The Original classic tour takes you through the brand's history and the whiskey they craft. Enjoy the complimentary whiskey tasting at the end of the tour. Admission from €8.00. Before you leave, you might like to visit the gift shop and browse for a memento to take back home.

CASTLETOWN HOUSE
Celbridge,
Co. Kildare
Tel: +353 1 628 8252
Fax: +353 1 627 1811
www.castletown.ie
Email:castletown@opw.ie

Ireland's first and finest 18th century Palladian style mansion on the banks of the River Liffey, just 20km from Dublin city. Free parking: Exit 6, M4, Celbridge West. Free admission to the Park and Riverside walks.

BATTLE OF THE BOYNE
Oldbridge
Drogheda
Co. Meath
Contact No: +353 41 9809950
Fax No: +353 41 9849873
Email: battleoftheboyne@opw.ie
Web: www.battleoftheboyne.ie

The Battle of the Boyne between King William III and his father-in-law, King James II, was fought on 1 July 1690 (11 July according to our modern calendar). Both kings commanded their armies in person, 36,000 on the Williamite side and 25,000 on the Jacobite side - the largest number of troops ever deployed on an Irish battlefield.

BRÚ NA BÓINNE VISITOR CENTRE
(Newgrange and Knowth)
Donore, Co. Meath
Contact No: +353 41 9880300
Fax No: +353 41 9823071
Email: brunaboinne@opw.ie
Web: www.heritageireland.ie

Brú na Bóinne Visitor Centre interprets the Neolithic monuments of Newgrange, Knowth and Dowth. The extensive exhibition includes a full scale replica of the chamber at Newgrange as well as a full model of one of the smaller tombs at Knowth.

GLENDALOUGH VISITOR CENTRE
Glendalough, Bray
Co Wicklow
Contact No: +353 404 45325/45352
Fax: +353 404 45626
Email: george.mcclafferty@opw.ie
Web: www.heritageireland.ie

This early Christian ecclesiastical settlement was founded by St. Kevin in the 6th century. Set in a glaciated valley with two lakes, the monastic remains include a superb round tower, stone churches and decorated crosses. The Visitor Centre has an interesting exhibition and an audio-visual show.

TRIM CASTLE
Trim,Co Meath
Contact No: +353 46 9438619
Fax No: +353 46 9438618
Email: trimcastle@opw.ie
Web: www.heritageireland.ie

Trim Castle, the largest Anglo-Norman castle in Ireland, was constructed over a thirty-year period by Hugh de Lacy and his son Walter. Construction of the massive three storied Keep, the central stronghold of the castle, was begun c. 1176 on the site of an earlier wooden fortress.

TULLAMORE D.E.W. VISITOR CENTRE
Bury Quay, Tullamore, Co. Offaly
Tel: +353 57 9325015
Fax: +353 57 93 25016
Email:info@tullamoredew.com
Web: www.tullamoredewvisitorcentre.com

Situated right in the heart of Ireland, there is an incredible experience that has been waiting for you since 1829. Join us at the newly renovated home of Tullamore D.E.W. Irish Whiskey and immerse yourself in the history and magic that lies inside the walls of this 19th century bonded warehouse, where our whiskey making tradition began. Enjoy a guided tour and a tutored whiskey tasting.

The Dublin Docklands

The City Centre boasts a selection of quality hotels which have been part of the Dublin landscape for many years, including the world famous **Shelbourne** on St. Stephens Green, **The Westbury, The Fitzwilliam** all within close proximity to the hub of Grafton Street. Also recommended are the **Merrion Hotel** on Merrion Street close to Government buildings and the **Conrad** on Earlsford Terrace opposite the National Concert Hall.

For a taste of five star luxury, stay at **The Westbury Hotel** on Grafton Street. Enjoy a warm welcome and relax in the magnificent setting of The Gallery and dine in one of their two fine restaurants. Right outside your door is the heart of Dublin City's cultural quarter with all the shops and pubs one could want.

The Camden Court Hotel is a modern 3 star hotel located in Dublin city centre. The hotel is just a short and pleasant walk from St Stephens Green and Grafton Street.

The Croke Park Hotel is a luxury hotel situated across the road from Croke Park Stadium. It is the preferred business and leisure hotel for GAA enthusiasts.

The 4 Star **Hilton Dublin Kilmainham Hotel** enjoys expansive views over the neighbouring Phoenix Park. Dine in the contemporary and stylish Cinnamon Restaurant. You could also consider **Jurys Inn Custom House** in the International Financial Services Centre (IFSC). The LUAS and Connolly Rail Station are just around the corner.

The **O'Callaghan Mont Clare** is a classically decorated, traditional 3 star Dublin hotel and a former favourite of James Joyce, nestled away in a peaceful Georgian Merrion Square.

The 4 star **O'Callaghan Alexander Hotel** is a hidden gem located in Dublin 2 within strolling distance of Grafton Street, Merrion Square and Trinity College. The **O'Callaghan Davenport Hotel** is a traditional elegant hotel with a historic facade that dates back to 1863. The Davenport is a well-known Dublin landmark.

Also in Dublin 2 is **Buswells**, an elegant and charming 67 bedroom, 3 star, Georgian hotel with special character.

Enjoy a delicious meal in **Thornton's** Michelin Star Restaurant in the 5 star **The Fitzwilliam Hotel**, St. Stephen's Green and relax afterward in the Inn On the Green Bar.

Ideal for your business or leisure needs is **The Gresham Hotel** situated on O' Connell Street and is close to the shopping district of Dublin.

The Westin Dublin, a luxury 5 star hotel, is located directly opposite Trinity College. Dine in the beautiful Atrium Lounge with its five–storey high glass ceiling.

The Arlington Hotel, located beside O' Connell Bridge along the River Liffey is world famous for its Celtic Rhythm Irish Dancing Night, while **The Arlington Hotel Temple Bar** offers 3 Star accommodation situated opposite Dublin Castle.

Or you could try the international award–winning 4 star **Ashling Hotel** adjacent to Heuston Station and on the Luas red line.

Right in the heart of Temple Bar you will find **The Riverhouse Hotel**. All of the rooms are tastefully decorated in a modern style with the emphasis on comfort. **Blooms Hotel** is a beautiful hotel with a charming atmosphere. Blooms also boasts one of the more popular nightclubs in Dublin, **Club M**, as well as the busy **VAT house Bar**. The **Temple Bar Hotel** is one of the city's most centrally located hotels in the cultural and entertainment heart of Dublin.

Also in Temple Bar on the banks of the River Liffey, you will find **Fitzsimons Hotel**, a boutique hotel situated in the heart of Temple Bar. Its location offers the visitor doorstep access to this vibrant, exciting locale and all it has to offer: theatres, galleries, bars, restaurants, live music venues and also alternative shops. Fitzsimons offers visitors a great place to socialise now with 5 floors of entertainment including their open air Roof Terrace with bar, bars on all floors, restaurant and nightclub, seven nights a week. At the Fitzsimons Hotel, they cater for a wide variety of visitors who pass through Temple Bar every year. Their level of service and customer commitment ensures that visitors return year after year.

If you require accommodation near the airport, there are a number of options. Located within the Dublin Airport complex, **The Clarion Hotel** is only 3 minutes from Terminal Two and is accessible by 24 hour coach pickup from the Airport. The four star **Radisson Blu Hotel** appeals to business and leisure travellers, providing elite access to the passenger terminal located just steps from the hotel.

Located on 85 acres of the mature woodlands of Northwood Park, Santry is the **Crowne Plaza Hotel Northwood**, a great Dublin Airport Hotel. **The Hilton Dublin Airport Hotel** offers nine flexible meeting rooms for up to 350 Guests, with WiFi and breakout rooms. Just a 10 minute drive from the airport is **The Best Western Dublin Skylon Hotel**, a modern, luxurious 126 bedroom hotel boasting free Wi-Fi and all non-smoking bedrooms.

LISTINGS

FITZSIMONS HOTEL TEMPLE BAR
21-22 Wellington Quay
Temple Bar, Dublin 2.
Tel: 00 353 1 6779315
Fax: 00 353 1 6779387
Email: info@fitzsimonshotel.com
Web: www.fitzsimonshotel.com

Fitzsimons Hotel (3 star) overlooking the River Liffey & located in the heart of Temple Bar, walking distance to all major Dublin attractions. Rooms with Flat screen TV's, river views & private balconies available. Bar, Nightclub & Restaurant on site with entertainment 7 nights.

Moving Southside, stay at **The Ballsbridge Hotel**, Dublin 4 and enjoy a relaxing meal in The Dubliner Pub or a more formal dining experience in Raglan's Restaurant. **The Clyde Court Hotel** formerly **The Berkley Court Hotel** offers deluxe rooms and fine dining in The Clyde, one of Dublin's most prestigious restaurants.

Also in Ballsbridge in the heart of the business and embassy district and next door to the RDS is **Bewley's Hotel Ballsbridge**.

Across the road is the 5 star **Four Seasons Dublin** which is an elegant hotel with spacious rooms, a range of bar and dining options, in a gorgeous, tranquil setting. You could also consider relaxing in luxury accommodation at the **Herbert Park Hotel** and take in the views over Herbert Park and Ballsbridge.

The Burlington Hotel is the largest conference hotel in Dublin City, just a short stroll from the RDS and the city centre. Within easy walking distance to the city's museums, galleries and shops is **The Grand Canal Hotel Dublin**, a modern, comfortable hotel.

Dating from 1750, the estate and mansion incorporating the **Radisson Blu St. Helen's Hotel** is only a short walk from University College Dublin. Also, **The Stillorgan Park Hotel** is one of Dublin's premier 4 star Fáilte Ireland and Automobile Association (AA) rated hotels.

In **Killiney Castle Hotel,** you will enjoy 18th century, four star castle accommodation in a tranquil atmosphere.

Bridges over
The Liffey

Pubs in Dublin

When it comes to Dublin, "are you going for a pint?" is not just a question, it's an order! With Irish theme bars taking over every city across the globe, why not go back to basics and savour the sights, sounds and smells of an authentic Dublin pub?

The official opening hours of pubs in Ireland are 10.30am to 11.30pm, Mondays to Thursdays and 10.30am to 12.30 am, Fridays and Saturdays and 12.00pm to 11.00pm on Sundays. Many pubs in the city centre have been granted later licences at weekends. For a dawn tipple, try the 'early houses' around **Smithfield** fruit market.

If Dublin is the heartland of Ireland, **Temple Bar** is surely its pulse. With many and varied outlets fighting for your attention, Temple Bar is a flurry of excitement, entertainment and anticipation. **The Temple Bar** is one of the liveliest pubs in this area, hosting two or more scheduled and impromptu 'trad' sessions a day. Voted Traditional Pub of the Year 2002 and 2003, it offers a spacious beer garden which has proved popular since the introduction of the smoking ban in March 2004.

Also in Temple Bar is **Fitzsimons Bar**. Located in **Fitzsimons Hotel**, it has free, live traditional music and late night entertainment. It also offers the luxury of a large screen for watching live sporting events, a definite asset in a sports mad city. This hotel also has a lively and popular

McDAIDS PUB

Established in 1779, **McDaids** is situated off
fashionable Grafton Street close to Dublin city centre.
One of the true literary pubs off Dublin it was
frequented by many of the greats of Irish literature,
including Patrick Kavanagh and Brendan Behan.
Today McDaids retains much of the character of an
earlier age whilst managing to maintain its tradition of
hospitality. Purveyors of fine beverages. Popular with
locals and tourists alike.

3 HARRY STREET, DUBLIN 2.
TEL: 01 6794395
olivercosgrave@hotmail.com

Guinness
and oysters

nightclub with nights hosted by some of Dublin's top DJs.

Blooms Hotel's VAT house Bar is a traditional pub which gets its name from the vat house in **Guinness Brewery**. Its warm and also relaxed atmosphere is complimented by a fine pint of 'the black stuff'.

McDaids is a classic pub on Harry Street (just off Grafton Street) and across from the Westbury Hotel. McDaids has proven to be very popular with tourists and locals alike, serving a selection of beers, with their Guinness second to none. A traditional Dublin pub, McDaids has been frequented by many of the literary greats such as Brendan Behan, Liam O' Flaherty and Patrick Kavanagh. With its distinctive Victorian exterior, this pub exudes old–style charisma. Famous guests include Hillary Clinton.

Other recommended locations in the Grafton Street area are **Nearys** on Chatham Street, **The Duke, The Bailey Bar and Davy Byrne's** on Duke Street. Davy Byrne's pub was a favourite of James Joyce and, perhaps more famously, of Leopold Bloom.

The Arlington Hotel O'Connell Bridge is one of the most centrally located hotels in Dublin city centre, offering superb accommodation in the very heart of the capital. The hotel has become world famous for its **Celtic Rhythm "Irish Dancing Night"**. The Arlington Hotel offers live Irish music and dancing, entertaining guests & visitors 7 nights week.

If you're seeking a traditional Irish music pub, then look no further than **McNeills** on Capel Street. McNeills was originally a celebrated music shop, operating from 148 Capel Street in 1834. Six years later, the business moved to number 137 before settling in a couple of doors down at number 140 in 1842. It traded from this spot for 162

FITZSIMONS
TEMPLE BAR

ROCK & POP Acts · **11.00 'til LATE** · **7 Nights**

8.30pm
Sunday
Monday
Tuesday
Wednesday
& Thursday

Times subject to change

FRIDAY & SATURDAY | Rock & Pop
LIVE BANDS

FITZ FREAKIN FRIDAY

9.00pm **Support Act**

11.30pm **MAIN BAND**

FOLLOWED BY
DJ 'til LATE on 5 floors

5 FLOOR SATURDAY

5ive Nightclub | From **11.00**pm | Guest DJs nightly · Chart Dance RnB and Pop · 7 Nights

Fitzsimons ROOF-TOP TERRACE Bar ┆ **7 Days**

Temple Bar, Dublin 2. T: 677 9315. F: 677 9387. E: info@fitzsimonshotel.com
www.fitzsimonshotel.com • www.facebook.com/fitzsimonsbar

The Gaiety
Theatre

years when it closed. Drop in any day of the week and enjoy the nightly, live, traditional Irish music sessions.

Late Night Entertainment

Late bars have become a popular option in Dublin and there is a fine variety to choose from ranging from jazz to Irish traditional music to dance and pop. Themed venues are sprouting up around the city centre.

The multi–level **Messrs Maguire**, which includes its own microbrewery, should not be missed. If jazz and blues are your fancy, **JJ Smyth's** on Aungier Street is worth a visit.

Club Nassau is home of the slow set and Dublin's original 80's Nightclub every Friday, Saturday and Bank Holiday Sunday night. With 2 floors, 2 dancefloors and also 4 bars including upstairs seating and air conditioning, this is the perfect place for a night of socialising.

City centre locations that should feature high on your list of nightclub priorities are **Club M** in Bloom's Hotel in Temple Bar, one of the most popular nights–out in Dublin and **Bobs**, formerly known as **Bad Bobs**, also in Temple Bar, which is a refurbished, multi–storied pub with plenty of atmosphere. For something original, try the cabaret–style **Sugar Club** on Leeson Street.

For evening entertainment, you should also consider the **Fitzwilliam Card Club** where you will experience the thrills of playing the casino in comfortable surroundings. It is located in Clifton Hall, Fitzwilliam Street in the heart of Dublin 2 and well–deserved of a visit.

McNeills Pub
& Music Sessions
Live traditional Irish music nightly from 9pm

McNeills Pub Sessions & Music Shop, located in Dublins city centre has been operating since 1834. The home of Traditional Irish Music in Dublin, live music runs nightly with some of the most infamous characters and musicians in the city sitting in on a regular basis. If you want to experience real traditional Irish culture in an original and comfortable setting then we would welcome your visit.

Established 1834 • Live Irish Music Nightly • No Cover Charge • Central Location
140 Capel Street, Dublin 1. Ph: +353 1 8747679
www.facebook.com/McNeillsPubSessions

The Blarney Inn is only minutes away from all the main attractions in Dublin. This pub serves a selection of traditional Irish food, a great pint of Guinness and their World Champion Irish Coffee as well as having regular live Irish music. Specials change daily so be sure to check out the diverse menu. You can't pack more Irishness into one spot.

For a lively atmosphere in modern surroundings, try **ely gastro bar** in Grand Canal Square. You will be spoiled for choice when it comes to food. The menu includes Irish lobster pot, Irish guinea fowl terrine and duo of organic Burren lamb. To quench your thirst, try the traditional homemade lemonade or sample their excellent cocktails, beers and wine.

You should also visit the newly renovated, contemporary **Mao** restaurants in Dun Laoghaire, Dundrum or Chatham Row to enjoy an extensive Asian menu and sample a cocktail or two. Kids are always welcome. If you fancy a night in, order from **Mao At Home** and bring all the same great Thai and Asian flavour straight to your door. The chefs use only the freshest of ingredients. Order from the Baggot Street, Donnybrook or Tallaght branches.

Try the **Hard Rock Cafe** and **TGI Fridays** for a lively dinner and cocktails to kick–start a night out. Enjoy mouth watering food in a chilled out environment in the Hard Rock Cafe. Sit back and enjoy the most up–to–date and cutting edge music and videos. Also the merchandise store on the ground floor of the restaurant sells Hard Rock Cafe collectibles, including souvenir glasses and teddy bears.

The atmosphere is always buzzing in **TGI Fridays**. Mix and match with appetizers to share, including their championship wings coated in BBQ and Jack Daniel's sauces, tostado nachos and buffalo wings. Wash them down with a refreshing beer or smoothie.

Outside the city centre, **Johnnie Fox's** must be experienced. Situated in Glencullen on top of the Dublin mountains, Johnnie Fox's is one of Ireland's oldest and most famous traditional Irish pubs – and they are also famed as the highest pub in the country. At Johnnie Fox's they have Live Irish Music seven nights a week. You can also see one of the top dancing performances in the country at their famous dinner & show – Hooley Night. Their award – winning seafood restaurant is open daily.

The Merry Ploughboy Pub, which first opened its doors in the early 1730's, prides itself as being one of the best places in Dublin to experience Irish Culture and genuine Irish hospitality to this very day. The pub also exclusively hosts the **"Merry Ploughboy Traditional nights"**, a highly entertaining night of Irish music, song and dance. The show runs seven nights per week, and practically all year round.

Theatres
Dublin's leading theatres include **The Gate**, on Parnell Square, and **The Abbey** at 26 Lower Abbey Street, which opened its doors to the public on Monday 18 July 1966, heralding the beginning of a new era for the National Theatre of Ireland. **The Peacock Theatre** lies beneath the Abbey foyer and the entrance is also on Lower Abbey Street.

The Olympia, located on Dame Street, is one of the oldest surviving theatres in Dublin and hosts a variety of shows from musicals to plays. **The Ark** in Temple Bar is Europe's first cultural centre for children with a gallery, workshop and theatre.

The National Concert Hall on Earlsfort Terrace, just off St Stephen's Green, is one of Europe's leading concert venues where many of the world's top artists have performed. Home to the RTÉ National Symphony Orchestra, the Hall hosts a variety of concerts, operas and musicals as well as lunchtime recitals.

The Gaeity Theatre on South King Street opened in 1871. For well over a century it has provided the people of the city with opera, musicals, drama, festivals and more. International stars such as Julie Andrews, Spike Mulligan and Joan Rivers have graced the theatre, as well as Irish stars like The Dubliners and The Chieftains. Keep an eye on the website for upcoming events.

As a Town Centre, **Dundrum** is also home to a wide range of leisure activities such as the 200 seat Mill Theatre, the 12 screen Movies@Dundrum cinema complex, the Rainforest indoor golfing range the fun Giddy Studios pottery making studio and the host of other activities that take place throughout the year such as fashion shows in Spring Summer and Autumn Winter and The Dundrum Ice Rink which arrives to Dundrum for 3 months of the year, not to mention the free kids activities which fill the summer holiday breaks. All information is available on the website www.dundrum.ie

For alternative entertainment a visit to **Shelbourne Park Greyhound Stadium** is well–recommended. Whether it's corporate entertainment or a night out with friends, enjoy a delicious meal at Dobbins grand–stand restaurant with pivotal views of the racing circuit guaranteeing you a great night out.

Harold's Cross is another superb purpose built facility boasting top notch food and guaranteeing a fun night out. The Irish Greyhound Board is a commercial semi– state body which is responsible for the control and development of the greyhound industry in the Republic of Ireland.

Casinos
The private members Casino and Card Club, **The Sporting Emporium**, caters to all types of players, from complete beginners to those who like to play for higher stakes. It is located over three floors just off Dublin's Grafton

LISTINGS

THE FITZSIMONS HOTEL
21-22 Wellington Quay, Dublin 2
Tel: +353 1 677 9315
Fax: 01-6779387
Email: info@fitzsimonshotel.com
Web: www.fitzsimonshotel.com
facebook.com/FitzsimonsBar

Dublin's No.1 Party Venue on 5 Floors, late 7 nights. BARS: live rock n pop music bar and live traditional Irish music and dancing. NIGHTCLUB: with chart music + DJ's. Food served daily. ROOF TOP TERRACE BAR: Dublin's only open air roof top bar.

Street and recently won the prestigious 'Best Casino Club' award. Enjoy Poker, Blackjack, Roulette, Brag, Punto Banco and 300 online casino games.

Family Entertainment
St. Patrick's Festival takes place all over Dublin city centre every year from around 11th–17th March. It is one of the main events of the Dublin calendar year and which the Dubliners are very proud of. The festival reaches its climax on St. Patrick's Day with a carnival parade through the city centre.

For a fun day out with family or friends, visit **Kylemore Indoor Karting**. This is Ireland's largest indoor Karting arena with a choice of three 360 mtr tracks with flyovers, underpasses, hills and banked corners. Kylemore Karting was established in 1992 as the first indoor track in the Republic of Ireland, and is now the country's market leader in indoor Karting. Experience the thrill of real racing!

LISTINGS

McDAIDS PUB 3 Harry Street, Dublin 2 Tel: 01 6794395 Email: olivercosgrave@hotmail.com	Established in 1779, McDaids is situated off fashionable Grafton Street near Dublin city centre. One of the true literary pubs it was frequented by many of the greats of Irish literature, including Patrick Kavanagh and Brendan Behan. McDaids retains its tradition of hospitality and is popular with locals and tourists alike. Purveyors of fine beverages.
McNeills Pub & Music Hall. 140 Capel Street, Dublin 1. Tel: 018747679. Web: www.facebook.com/McNeillsPubSessions	Established in 1834 McNeills has long been a home of traditional Irish music and the original example of the true Irish pub. With open music sessions from 9pm nightly and no cover charge, this is a pub to visit to experience real Irish culture in front of a proper turf fire.
SHELBOURNE PARK GREYHOUND STADIUM South Lotts Road, Ringsend, Dublin 4 Tel: 1890-269-969 Fax: 01 6683246 Email: sales@igb.ie Web: www.shelbourneparkgreyhoundstadium.ie	A perfect location whatever the occasion be it a family or work outing, Corporate event or simply a night out with friends. Racing every Wednesday, Thursday and Saturday (additional Friday nights racing in December). Packages available to suit all budgets. For reservations call 1890 269 969.

A NIGHT WITH A DIFFERENCE

SHELBOURNE PARK is the home of Greyhound Racing in Ireland and holds three action packed race nights every week, on Wednesday, Thursday and Saturday nights (additional Friday nights in December). Doors open at 6:30pm with the first race at appx 7:45pm each evening.

The stadium is located in Dublin on South Lotts Road, Ringsend, Dublin 4. There is even an excellent **FREE SHUTTLE SERVICE** provided by **DUBLIN COACH** on a Saturday night by that leaves from D'Olier street in the heart of the city centre at 7pm and returns you there after the last race at 10:30pm.

FREE SHUTTLE

EVERY SATURDAY
▶ Pick Up at D'Olier Street every Saturday @ 7.00pm
▶ Departing Stadium at 10.30pm

To immerse yourself in an activity steeped in Irish culture, there's no better choice and value than a night at the Irish Greyhound Board's flagship stadium, Shelbourne Park.

If you've never experienced greyhound racing before then its time you came up to speed! Nothing beats the flutter of excitement as you place your bet; the rush of adrenaline as you see your dog sprinting from the traps or the sheer exhilaration of watching your dog cross the finish line in pole position.

The stadium offers luxurious facilities with superb dining options, buzzing bars and great value packages to suit all budgets and tastes. There are **MIDWEEK RESTAURANT PACKAGES** from as little as €29.99 p/person. This includes admission and racecard, reserved seating in our Dobbins Grandstand Restaurant which offers Panoramic views of the track, a 4 course meal and tableside tote and bar service.

Group Packages start from as little as €12.50 p/person on our hugely popular **SHELBOURNE PARTY PACK DEAL**. This includes admission and racecard (normally €10), Dobbins Jumbo Sausage and Chips, €2 tote voucher and €2 drink voucher. Challenging in the popularity stakes is the incredible value for money **DOBBINS PLATTER DEAL** at only €15 p/person. This includes admission and racecard and a delicious selection of Dobbins party favourites designed to share. There are also 7 superb private suite facilities, complete with private bar and tote services and with a range of cocktail, buffet and dining menus starting from as little as €25 p/person (min numbers apply on all group packages).

It really is a great value night out with a difference so whether its business or pleasure, make it your business to get to Shelbourne Park for an unforgettable night at the dogs.

BOOKING IS EASY...

Reservations call **1890 269 969**

Or book online **www.Shelbourneparkgreyhoundstadium.ie**

SHELBOURNE PARK
GREYHOUND STADIUM

Irish cooking has traditionally emphasised the use of fresh, local ingredients cooked with a minimum of fuss. A new generation of Irish chefs continues to make a virtue of this simplicity; many menus are based on fresh seafood and locally sourced meat and vegetables.

But, as well as modern Irish cuisine, the foods of many nations now compete for the diner's attention. Book your table ahead of time in Dublin – a requirement more so here than in most cities of comparable size – especially at weekends and during the summer.

Popular outdoor lunchtime hang-outs in good weather are the **Liffey Boardwalk**, St Stephen's Green, the lawn beside the Arts Block at Trinity College, or also the beautiful secluded **Iveagh Gardens** off Earlsfort Terrace.

The 3 **ely** restaurants specialise in sourcing the very best organic beef, lamb and pork. In fact they only use 3 farmers and 2 butchers to supply all their meats. Since 1999 ely has always sourced fresh Irish chicken and seafood and its seasonal Irish fruit and vegetables are grown less than an hour away. Their organic pork and

ely wine bar, 22, Ely Place, Dublin 2

beef comes from their own farm and their wild venison comes from the father of one of their chefs. They also make and bake everything in house. Add in almost a hundred wines by the glass, craft beers, great cocktails and friendly staff and look forward to a great visit to Dublin. So be sure to pay a visit to **ely bar and brasserie** in the Irish Financial Services Centre, **ely winebar** in the heart of Georgian Dublin and **ely gastro bar** in Grand Canal Square.

The Epicurean Food Hall in the city centre is a collection of food shops & counters with communal seating offering a variety of healthy, multi–

cultural meals. The atmosphere is always buzzing as visitors enjoy the ethnic cafes and little shops.

Why not sample some of the city's rock culture at the **Hard Rock Café**. From fantastic memorabilia, fabulous drinks and great American food and service it has everything you're looking for and is also centrally located. Opened in 2004, Dublin's **Hard Rock** offers a selection of American cuisine and excellent cocktails. Like all Hard Rock Cafes, Dublin's restaurant hosts an impressive collection of memorabilia including a pair of Bono's sunglasses, also a favourite shirt of Elvis's and a Jimi Hendrix rug. Food and drinks are excellent and you can't beat the friendly and relaxed atmosphere.

Other American style restaurants include **T.G.I. Friday's,** found at centres around the city, including St Stephen's Green, Blanchardstown, Temple Bar, Dundrum Town Centre and Swords. Serving mouth watering burgers, steaks and a huge range of exotic cocktails, it is the ideal venue for a night out or a family gathering. For quality American food served in a fun atmosphere look no further than TGI Friday's. It's the perfect place to unwind after a hard day's sight-seeing.

At **Mao** restaurants located in Dun Laoghaire, Dundrum and in the heart of the city at Chatham Row, the chefs are passionate about using only the finest fresh ingredients to create authentic, virtually low fat Thai/Asian dishes. Try the Five Spice Chicken, Nasi Goreng and Black Pepper Beef. All dishes are prepared using only 100% Irish beef.

If you would prefer the same tempting food brought directly to your door, there's **Mao at Home**. You can order online or by phone from branches at Baggot Street, Donnybrook and Tallaght. Try the Singapore Style Roasted Duck, Vegetarian Nasi Goreng and Chilli Chicken Ramen.

Captain Americas serve good quality American-style food at reasonable prices. In Dublin there are three branches

YAMAMORI

Yamamori offers an authentic Japanese cultural food experience, with 19th Century Japanese artefacts and artworks throughout the venues. After nineteen years as Dublin's first ever Japanese restaurant, Yamamori is now Europe's largest Japanese food provider, and offers 3 characteristic restaurants and 2 lively sake bars.

Whether it be a comforting bowl of chunky aromatic noodles in Yamamori Noodles, a sunny afternoon enjoying the freshest sushi in the Bamboo Garden at Yamamori Sushi, or dancing the night away with spicy fruit cocktails at Izakaya and Tengu, Yamamori has something for everyone!

*" Yamamori rarely disappoints
with its bubbly service
and vivacious cooking "*
(TheLonelyPlanet)

www.yamamorisushi.ie

✄--✄

COUPON

One complimentary dessert when you buy any main course.

This coupon is for one person only, valid January to December 2015.

✄--✄

in Grafton Street, Tallaght and also Blanchardstown, all serving delicious food and an extensive selection of cocktails, beers and wines. Try the loaded potato skins, New York Sirloin Steak or the chicken and cheese enchilada.

For a taste of Asian cuisine, visit any of the **Wagamama** noodle bars located in South King Street, Dundrum Town Centre and Blanchardstown Retail Park. Relax in informal style and dine on noodles served with a variety of ingredients including chicken, shrimp, egg, bean–sprouts and peppers or try their big bowls of noodle soup.

Acapulco Mexican Restaurant on South Great Georges Street offers the best in traditional Mexican cuisine. Relax in this authentic and lively restaurant and choose from a variety of dishes including burritos, nachos, pizza mexicana, enchiladas, spicy chicken fajitas and chilli del diable. For a special treat order a pitcher of margarita to share with your table or simply enjoy a Corona or choose a glass of red or white from the wine menu.

If it's real Irish fare you're after, **Boxty** in Temple Bar serves traditional dishes such as their Irish lamb and beef stews, traditional corned beef and bacon ribs. Try their Famous Gaelic Boxty, tender medallions of Irish fillet beef in a whiskey and mushroom cream sauce wrapped in traditional Leitrim Boxty Pancake. The restaurant celebrates the finest of traditions in Irish cuisine in an atmosphere that is contemporary and timeless, cosmopolitan and nostalgic.

Food and Drink in a Dublin Pub

LE BON CRUBEEN & THE CELT

RESTAURANT - WINE BAR AND TRADITIONAL IRISH PUB

OPEN SEVEN DAYS FROM 12PM
UNTIL VERY LATE

CLOSE TO THE ABBEY, GATE
& O2 THEATRES

Lunch every day. Early Bird / Pre-Theatre from 5pm.

€25 value dinner three courses all night all week from 5pm.

Le Jazz Supper from 9pm to very late on Saturday nights.

Voted No 1 Restaurant
for food, service
and value

LE BON CRUBEEN
RESTAURANT BAR

- TRADITIONAL IRISH PUB -

private dining | live jazz | lunch | brunch | pre-theatre | dinner

TEL: 01 704 0126

81-82 TALBOT STREET, DUBLIN CITY CENTRE

info@leboncrubeen.ie   www.leboncrubeen.ie

Also a must stop is **Oliver St John Gogarty's Bar & Restaurant** where a carvery lunch operates daily until 3.30pm, after which an extensive bar food menu takes over. A sample of Ireland's traditional music scene is also available.

For a taste of Italy, visit **Pacino's Restaurant, Bar & Venue** beside Trinity College Dublin on Suffolk Street for breakfast, lunch or dinner, or simply enjoy their range of Cicchetti (small snacks or side dishes). Order a glass of white, red or rosé wine or try a draught beer. Relax in the rustic atmosphere complemented by the finest authentic rustic Italian food.

La Mere Zou, Les Fréres Jacques and **Salamanca** all offer the best of our continental cousins and are conveniently located in the city centre. **L'Ecrivain,** which is situated on Lower Baggot Street, is one of only six Michelin – starred Irish restaurants, and the place food critics rave about.

Coppinger Row is a Mediterranean restaurant in the heart of the most thriving part of the city centre. They are nestled in the pedestrian lane of Coppinger Row in close proximity to landmark locations such as Dublin Castle, Trinity College and Grafton St., Dublin's most famous shopping thoroughfare. Coppinger Row produces the best quality, simply prepared

Mediterranean food at the right price in a space that is relaxed, vibrant and fun.

For a authentic taste of Mexican cuisine, try **Tuzo Mexican Kitchen** on Dawson Street. Enjoy burritos, fajitas, tacos and salads or a bowl of chilli in this authentic cantina in Dublin city centre. If it's a small snack you're after, you can't go wrong with some chips topped with guacamole or salsa. Don't forget to order a Margarita or Corona with your meal.

And for a range of standard and more unusual Chinese food, drop in to **The Good World Chinese Restaurant** on South Great Georges Street. This great restaurant is very popular with the local Chinese, and the service is fast and efficient. The menu suits both Chinese and also European customers. And of special interest on the menu is the selection of Dim Sums.

La Dolce Vita

Situated in the heart of historical Dublin, across the road from the Kilmainham jail, and the museum of Modern Art, La Dolce Vita Restaurant features beautiful views which overlook the former courthouse and the famous Dublin streets. Our food offers an authentic Irish/Italian dining experience at terrific value! Open from midday until eleven p.m every day.

LA DOLCE VITA RESTAURANT
760 South circular road
Kilmainham, Dublin 8
Tel: 01 6169581
Fax: 01 6169581
Email: mlenghel@yahoo.ie
Web: www.ladolcevita.ie

Darwins Restaurant is an award winning, family run business on Aungier Street. It prides itself on its certified Irish Angus beef and local produce. The theme of the restaurant is based on Charles Darwin's 'origin of the species'. Darwins own in-house butchers supply and source all their certified Irish meats including Angus, game, poultry and genuine Dry aged beef.

The Classic Irish Coffee available in most Bars and Restaurants

The Lobster Pot Restaurant in Ballsbridge blends old world charm with intimate surroundings. Owned by the Crean family for over 30 years, it is one of the longest running family restaurants in Ireland. This warm and very friendly, silver service restaurant offers an extensive selection of seafood sourced daily, Irish meats, free

range poultry and game when in season. Just some of the tasty dishes on offer are lightly Smoked Wild West Cork Salmon, Carlingford Oysters Natural, Fresh Onion Soup and Lobster Pot Seafood Chowder. The menu uses only the freshest of ingredients. There is also an impressive wine list and a full licensed bar.

Bringing authentic Japanese culture and cuisine to Dublin since 1995, **Yamamori** is the perfect place to experience a true taste of Japan. Based in 3 locations in the heart of Dublin City, Yamamori's expert chefs have been treating locals and tourists alike for over 19 years. This renowned restaurant with its bold black and red exterior features an extensive menu of fabulous, fresh Japanese food. Groups of all sizes gravitate to its long benches and tables while very efficient and friendly staff serve up traditional and inspired exotic eats. The vegetarian menu is just as fulfilling, with plenty alternative dishes for vegans too.

tuzo
mexican kitchen

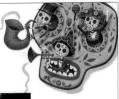

Opening Hours

Mon-Wed	11-9
Thur-Sat	11-10.30
Sun	1-8

www.tuzomex.com

The Lobster Pot
RESTAURANT

9 Ballsbridge Terrace, Ballsbridge, Dublin 4
Tel: +353 1 6680025 /6609170 Website: www.thelobsterpot.ie

Situated close to the American Embassy and within walking distance of many of Dublin's Leading hotels, *the Lobster pot* has been bringing a taste of the sea to Ballsbridge For 31years. Established in 1980, *The Lobster Pot Restaurant* is one of Dublin's best kept Dining secrets, blending an old world charm with intimate surroundings. We pride ourselves on an extensive selection of fresh Fish and Shellfish sourced daily, And indeed our equally noted meats, free range poultry and game in season.Choose from our extensive wine list which is sure to please the most refined of tastes. Freshness throughout is the key and we will assist your menu choice by presenting a fresh seafood display Tray to help answer any of your questions. Why not crown off your dining experience with crepes Suzette flambéed and a fine dessert wine, or if sweet is not for you how about a selection of Irish cheeses and a Tawny Port?

Visit our website to experience a flavour of what we have to offer.

Early Bird Mon – Fri
6pm – 7.30pm
2 Course €23.95
3 Course €26.95

Set Dinner Menu €39.50 all year round

Whether it be the 19th century artefacts, a comforting bowl of aromatic noodles, sushi in the sunny Bamboo Garden, or dancing the night away with fresh, sweet and spicy cocktails, Yamamori has something for everyone! "A real gem... this is sushi and fun all rolled into one!" (Inyourpocket.com).

The "chipper" (fish & chip shop) is a much-loved Irish institution and **Beshoffs** is one of the best known names in Dublin. Beshoffs which is located on 6–7 O' Connell Street takes pride in serving top quality fish and real potato chip meals in relaxed and comfortable surroundings. Friendly, quick service and affordable tasty food makes this a treat to visit.

The Gallery Restaurant at **The Church** is set on the mezzanine level with a stunning view overlooking the main bar. It offers world class food and very friendly service seven nights a week from 5pm. The restaurant also features the beautifully restored Renatus Harris built organ as its centre piece in the dining area.

For authentic Thai cuisine, **Diep** is the place to eat. At Diep Le Shaker on Pembroke Lane, try the Sai Krok Moo appetisers, Chiang Mai Pork lollipops with chilli, garlic, lime leaves, lettuce and tamarind. If a noodle bar is more your style, visit Diep Noodle Bar at Dublin Airport T2 and Mortons in Dublin 2 for Thai and also Vietnamese food. If you want to take Diep home with you, collection and delivery are available from several locations throughout Dublin including Blackrock, Dundrum and Blanchardstown.

The award-winning **Kilkenny Café** is located on the first floor of The **Kilkenny Shop**; it boasts beautiful views over the leafy grounds of Trinity College. They offer a splendid selection of hot food dishes, salads, pies, quiches, cakes and pastries are freshly made on site every morning. Gluten-free foods are available daily. Gourmet Breakfast Offer for €5 and Afternoon Sweet Treat Offer. Download their menu @ www.kilkennyshop.com

For a slice of Italian fine food and wines, a meal from the **Dunne & Crescenzi Group** of Italian restaurants is in order. Drop into any of their restaurants: Dunne & Crescenzi located in South Frederick Street and also Sandymount, Bar Italia, Ormond Quay and L'Officina in Dundrum Town Centre and Kildare Village. Enjoy pasta, risotto, antipasti, mouth watering desserts and much more.

For a little taste of Italy on South Circular Road in Kilmainham, try **La Dolce Vita**. All food and sauces are freshly prepared and cooked by their chef. Enjoy the delicious Chicken Dolce Vita, Magret Duck, Tortellini Ricotta & Spinach or Pizza Vesuvio. For dessert, try to decide between their strawberry cheesecake and tiramisu or simply opt for a selection of ice–cream.

Le Bon Crubeen is a restaurant and wine bar on Talbot Street and the 2010 winner of the Irish Restaurant Awards' Best Casual Dining Restaurant Dublin as well as Best

Traditional Irish Food
Smoked salmon, brown bread and a pint of Guinness

Value Restaurant Dublin in The Dubliner Top 100 restaurants 2012. If you are going to the nearby Abbey Theatre or The Gate Theatre after dinner, try their Pre-Theatre Menu and sample the Guinness brown bread, the beer battered fresh haddock or the crab and crayfish salad.

With 40 restaurants to choose from **Dundrum Town Centre** offers a very extensive dining offer with everything from the fine dining to the kids favourite, family friendly or perhaps just a coffee stop. Authentic Italian, Mexican, tapas, burgers and steaks that melt in the mouth. They have award– winning Indian food and Asian fusion and not forgetting that favourite cup of coffee with a little chocolate treat. For mouth–watering patisseries try The Bakery. Dundrum can cater for all you culinary desires.

A trip to the farm and gardens of Airfield in Dundrum is not complete without a stop for a bite to eat at **Overends.** The cafe, named after Letitia and Naomi Overend, provides delicious meals, taking inspiration from Airfield and its farm and gardens. Relax in a warm environment and enjoy a coffee with your meal. Airfield is only twenty minutes from the city centre on the Luas.

Outside the city, in Glencullen on top of the Dublin mountains, is **Johnnie Fox's** pub. Their award–winning –seafood kitchen offers fresh oysters, hand picked and opened to order, Irish smoked salmon, homemade "mountain" chowder, Fox's crab claws and much more.

Whatever your taste is in cuisine, diversity and choice are certainly on the menu wherever you might find yourself in Dublin.

ACAPULCO MEXICAN RESTAURANT
7 South Great Georges Street, Dublin 2
Tel: 01 677 1085
Web: www.acapulco.ie

Sizzling with all the exuberance of Latin America, enjoy fajitas, burritos, enchiladas, & other Mexican treats such as tacos with fresh soft corn tortillas (gluten free) and Margaritas made from 100% pure Agave Tequila. Delicious vegetarian options also available for practically every dish. Open for lunch and dinner.

BESHOFFS RESTAURANT
7 Upper O'Connell St,
Dublin 1
Tel: 01 8724400
Web: www.beshoffrestaurant.com

Beshoff's, 7 Upper O'Connell St. is a stones throw from the Spire. We take great pride in producing good quality Fish and real potato Chips. Relax in our comfortable surroundings with a great view of the city centre.

DARWIN'S RESTAURANT
80 Aungier street,
Dublin 2
Tel: 014757511
www.darwins.ie

Darwin's award winning, Irish family run restaurant, located in the city centre just 5 minutes from St. Stephen's green is held in high regard by many as being a chic and modern restaurant, serving an exciting range of food by warm and friendly staff. Well known for their steaks Darwin's also has a wide variety of fresh seafood and a full vegetarian menu available. The presentation of each dish provides a unique and unforgettable dining experience.

ely bar & brasserie
IFSC,
Dublin 1
Tel: 01 672-0010
Email: elybrasserie@elywinebar.com
Web: www.elywinebar.com

ely bar & brasserie, voted "Best Wine Bar in Ireland" 2014, is one of Dublin's most historical bars and restaurants. In a 200 year old converted wine & tobacco warehouse and situated on the waterfront in the IFSC, the stunning vaulted cellars offer the very best of fresh Irish produce, an award-winning wine list along with excellent craft beers and cocktails. This is a superb brasserie serving fresh Irish seafood, organic pork & lamb, dry-aged steaks and much more.

ely winebar
22, Ely Place,
Dublin 2
Tel: 01 676-8986
Email: elyplace@elywinebar.com
Web: www.elywinebar.com

The original provider of great wine by the glass, ely wine bar leads the way for Dublin wine bars. Awarded "Best Wine Experience in Ireland" 2014, their extensive and brilliantly chosen wine list is complimented by the very best of local organic Irish produce. Enjoy grass fed beef from ely's own organic family farm, the freshest Irish oysters or simply pop in for a cheeseboard and great glass of wine in Dublin's Iconic wine bar.

BOXTY
20 Temple Bar
Dublin 2
Tel: + 353 (0)1 677 2762
Email: info@boxtyhouse.ie
Web: www.boxtyhouse.ie
Twitter: @theboxtyhouse

Boxty has been at the beating heart of a dynamic, contemporary community for over 25 years. Our guests experience a genuine taste of modern Ireland, full of eclectic talking points and the warmth of that country kitchen down the west. The relaxed, warm atmosphere provides a natural habitat for conversation to flow easily and to share stories.

GOOD WORLD CHINESE RESTAURANT 18 South Great Georges Street, Dublin 2 Tel: 01 6775373	The restaurant has been established since 1991. Dim sum and Cantonese cuisine is what we do best. We offer lunch and early bird specials as well as a special dinner for two. We cater for large groups.
LA DOLCE VITA RESTAURANT 760 South circular road, Kilmainham, Dublin 8 Tel: 01 6169581 Fax: 01 6169581 Email: mlenghel@yahoo.ie Web: www.ladolcevita.ie	Situated in the heart of historical Dublin, across the road from the Kilmainham jail, and the museum of Modern Art, La Dolce Vita Restaurant features beautiful views which overlook the former courthouse and the famous Dublin streets. Our food offers an authentic Irish/Italian dining experience at terrific value! Open from midday until eleven p.m every day.
LE BON CRUBEEN 81/82 Talbot street Dublin 1 Tel: 01 7040126 Email: leboncrubeen@gmail.com Web: www.leboncrubeen.ie	Winner in 2010 and short-listed as finalist in 2012 of the Irish Restaurant Awards' Best Casual Dining Restaurant Dublin and winner of Best Value Restaurant Dublin in The Dubliner Top 100 restaurants 2012. Le Bon Crubeen's brasserie menu delivers a consistently great value dining experience all week long.
OVERENDS, AIRFIELD Overend Way, Dundrum, Dublin 14 Tel: 01 9696666 Email: info@airfield.ie Web: www.airfield.ie	The chefs at Overends take their inspiration directly from the produce of Airfield's farm and gardens that are then cooked simply to produce great tasting seasonal dishes, giving our diners the perfect experience of enjoying 'farm to fork' in a unique urban destination.
PACINO'S RESTAURANT, BAR & VENUE 18 Suffolk Street Dublin 2 Tel: 01 677 5651 Email: info@pacinos.ie Web: pacinos.ie	Pacino's Restaurant, Bar & Venue is ideally positioned on Suffolk Street, in Dublin's main retail and social district. We are located beside Trinity College Dublin, The Molly Malone Statue, beside the famous Grafton Street Shopping promenade and Dublin's Tourist Information Centre. Pacino's Restaurant, Bar & Venue is easy to find and close to all the main city centre attractions.
THE LOBSTER POT 9 Ballsbridge Terrace, Ballsbridge, Dublin 4 Tel: +353 1 6680025 /6609170 Website: www.thelobsterpot.ie	Blending old world charm with intimate surroundings, The Lobster Pot has been bringing a taste of the sea to Ballsbridge for 31 years. Choose from an extensive selection of fresh Fish and Shellfish sourced daily, equally noted meats, free range poultry and game when in season.

THE KILKENNY CAFE 6-15 Nassau Street Dublin 2 Tel: 01 677 7066 Email: info@kilkennygroup.com Web: www.kilkennyshop.com	The award-winning Kilkenny Café boasts beautiful views over the leafy grounds of Trinity College. A splendid selection of hot food dishes, salads, pies, quiches, cakes and pastries are freshly made on site every morning. Gourmet breakfast & Afternoon sweet treat offers.
TUZO MEXICAN KITCHEN 51b Dawson Street Dublin 2 Tel: 01 679 8814 Email: info@tuzomex.com Web: www.tuzomex.com F: /tuzomexdublin T: @tuzo_mex	Embrace the taste and spirit of Mexico at this authentic cantina in Dublin city centre. The finest ingredients and spices are slowly cooked to a secret recipe and served up in the best burritos in town. Fajitas, tacos and salads keep those full-on flavours coming.
YAMAMORI Noodles 72 South Great George's Street Dublin 2 Tel: (01) 872 0003 Email: info@yamamorinoodles.ie Web: www.yamamorinoodles.ie	Established in 1995, Dublin's first ever Japanese restaurant Yamamori Noodles has won numerous awards for quality food and service. Yamamori Noodles is the ideal restaurant for lunches, dinners, and parties.
YAMAMORI Sushi & Tengu 38/39 Lower Ormond Quay, Dublin 1 Tel: (01) 475 5001 Email: info@yamamorisushi.ie Web: www.yamamorisushi.ie	An authentic and cultural experience. Soak up the rays with some fresh sushi in the garden, bring your friends for dinner, or enjoy some beer and cocktails with Dublin's finest DJs in the Tengu Bar.
YAMAMORI Izakaya 12/13 South Great George's Street, Dublin 2 Tel: (01) 645 8001 Email: izakayadublin@gmail.com Web: www.yamamoriizakaya.ie	Enjoy an eclectic fusion of Japas dishes and sake. Taste the flavours of the Orient with a Spicy Asian Cocktail, and complete the night dancing to the music of Dublin's finest Djs at Yamamori Izakaya.

Kildare Village one of the Chic Outlet Shopping® Villages in Europe, is located less than an hour from Dublin and offers Ireland's only luxury outlet shopping experience. With designer boutiques providing fashion and luxuries for the home, **Kildare Village** offers authentic previous seasons' collections of a unique selection of Irish and international brands with savings of up to 60% on the recommended retail price, seven days a week and all year round.

Anya Hindmarch, Brooks Brothers, Cath Kidston, Church's, Coach, DKNY, Furla, Joules, Hugo Boss, Juicy Couture, L.K. Bennett, Pandora and Wolford are just a few of the international brands present, as well as the boutique of Ireland's leading international designer, Louise Kennedy.

A selection of services at **Kildare Village** includes a Tourist Information Centre; tax free shopping and a complimentary shuttle service to the nearby Irish National Stud & Gardens.

With a range of restaurants and cafés, the Village has become a destination for visitors seeking a superior shopping experience and an enjoyable day out.

For further information visit KildareVillage.com.

Curators of Style

LIKE SHOPPING. BUT BETTER.

The finest designer boutiques.
All in one place. With up to 60%* off.

ANYA HINDMARCH   BROOKS BROTHERS   CATH KIDSTON   FURLA
JOULES   LINKS OF LONDON   LOUISE KENNEDY   LULU GUINNESS
MOLTON BROWN AND MANY MORE

KILDARE VILLAGE
CHIC OUTLET SHOPPING®
KildareVillage.com

When it comes to the world fashion stakes and lists of shopping outlets, Dublin has previously never been high on people's agenda. However, with the influx of UK chain stores and large American–style shopping malls, the city's retailers offer ample opportunities for Dubliners to stretch their credit cards.

The main axis for the die-hard shopper is Grafton Street in the south city centre, which has been compared to London and New York in recent polls. It is also fully pedestrianised, and you are afforded a range of shops like the high–end Brown Thomas.

Brown Thomas is Ireland's premier luxury department store and part of a global retail family, which includes Selfridges in the UK and Holt Renfrew in Canada. Celebrating creativity, luxury and service since 1849, Brown Thomas is home to the very best Irish and international brands in fashion, accessories, beauty and home. Featuring the world's most prestigious luxury boutiques such as Cartier, Hermés, Chanel and Louis Vuitton, Brown Thomas Dublin has achieved pre–eminent status, a store that is listed among the best in the world, yet remains quintessentially Irish and unique. Visit www.brownthomas.com for more details.

Stephen's Green Shopping Centre

Just off the red brick carpet of Grafton Street you'll find the multi–storied **Stephen's Green Shopping Centre** and two smaller, but unique shopping complexes: **Powerscourt Townhouse Centre** and the **Royal Hibernian Way**.

Stephen's Green Shopping Centre is centrally located in the heart of the city at the top of **Grafton Street** and has over

one hundred shops all under one roof. There are a number of retail shops including **TK Maxx, Dunnes Stores** and **Swamp** as well as places to relax in after your shopping spree. Whether you're after a quiet coffee in a cafe, burger and chips in a fast food joint or a three course meal in a restaurant, you won't have to go far. For presents to take home to your loved ones, try **Celtic Spirit, The Donegal Shop, Carroll's Irish Gift Store** and **The Green Gallery.**

Powerscourt Townhouse Centre located on South William Street is a specialty shopping centre that offers a mixture of restaurants, art, antiques and fashion. In 1774 Richard Wingfield 3rd Viscount Powerscourt and his wife Lady Amelia moved into number 59 South William Street. The Townhouse with its history and shops, makes it well worth a visit. Open seven days a week. The Powerscourt Townhouse Centre is also home to the Design Centre, founded over 20 years ago. It became a forum for up and coming and established designers to showcase their clothing.

R & C McCormack is a family–run Jewellery shop on Grafton Street that prides itself on having the finest selection of Celtic Irish Jewellery including the traditional Irish ring of friendship, the Claddagh ring and Celtic Trinity Knot rings (the Trinity Knot is often found in Insular art such as metal work and in illuminated manuscripts like the Book of Kells). The staff are friendly and knowledgeable and the prices affordable for the high quality of the jewellery on offer.

NEW MOON
JEWELLERY

Located in the 19th century Victorian Georges Street Arcade, New Moon has Dublin's largest selection of hand made Sterling Silver, Gold and Gemstone jewellery.

New Moon Jewellery store has a mesmerizing collection of handmade sterling silver, gold and gemstone jewellery from around the world, all ethically sourced by owner Philippe Benaksas. Check out the huge range of silver pendants, rings, bangles and earrings set with rainbow moonstone, turquoise, amber, aquamarine, opal, topaz, tourmaline, garnet, ruby, jasper, kyanite, moldovite and many more rare stones. New Moon also has a large range of solid silver men's jewellery, from heavy snake chains to cufflinks, silver rings and bangles. Centrally located in the historic George's Street Arcade with friendly and knowledgeable staff on hand.

George's Street Arcade offers old world charm in this Victorian shopping mall that was Dublin's first shopping centre. This lively indoor market offers an abundance of charming shops and stalls in a unique bohemian atmosphere and is perfect for some exotic gift options. An eclectic and also unique shopping experience in the heart of Dublin city.

Located on Dawson Street and full of small, stylish shops, **Royal Hibernian Way** is a must see. If you'd like to take home a bottle of the 'good stuff', the **Celtic Whiskey Shop**, just around the corner, sells a fine selection of Irish, Scottish, Bourbon and world whiskeys as well as offering free whiskey tastings. Located at 27–28 Dawson Street, it is managed by Alastair Alpine who has over twenty years experience in the trade.

The Great Irish Shopping Experience can also be discovered on Nassau Street opposite Trinity College, where you will find **House of Ireland, The Kilkenny Store and Celtic Note**.

The beautiful **Kilkenny Shop** is famous for promoting Irish design and crafts for over 50 years – located just opposite Trinity College this is a must see while in Dublin. Offering a vast array of Waterford crystal, pottery, linen, jewellery, fashion, accessories and souvenirs you are sure to find the perfect gift at Kilkenny. Get crystal engraved free of charge, avail of shipping promotions, tax free shopping & a complimentary gift wrapping service. Upstairs is the fabulous Kilkenny Café – delicious homemade delights served daily!

The Sweater Shop stores are Irish owned and are proud to provide a vast selection of quality Irish Knitwear such as Aran jumpers, at great prices, as well as accessories, gifts and stylish casual wear. **The Sweater Shop** are also proud owners of **Trinity Sweaters** and **Trinity Crafts,** located directly opposite Trinity College. In their stores you will find a large selection of merchandise to suit all tastes. **Trinity Crafts** is also the official stockist of **Dublin Harley Davidson** clothing.

Muji on Chatham Street opened its doors in 2002. It is a Japanese store selling stylish furniture and an array of accessories for a modern lifestyle. They stock a wide range of products including stationery, storage, fashion and accessories, furniture, travel, health and beauty and kitchenware. Muji is open seven days a week.

THE SHOPPING CENTRE OF DUBLIN

Since opening its doors 26 years ago in 1988, **Stephen's Green Shopping Centre** has welcomed and encouraged millions of people to take advantage of its unique and diverse shopping experience. From independent boutiques to internationally loved brands and some of the best bars and restaurants in town, **Stephen's Green Shopping Centre** has something for everyone.

Its Victorian greenhouse style design, with thousands of panes of glass, pitched glass roof and viewing platforms gives shoppers a more relaxed and enjoyable shopping experience. The glass dome, which sits above the centre's doors, has become an iconic city landmark, perched in the skyline, it is easily identifiable for both tourists and Dubliners alike.

An extremely popular tourist destination, with it's close proximity to many bus routes, the Luas Green Line and Saint Stephen's Green itself, the shopping centre also acts as the gateway to the hustle of Grafton Street and the bustle of the city centre. It's hard to believe that this shopping centre, which is now so well established in the minds and memories of the locals, was nothing more than a derelict car park and rundown market only 27 years ago.

Stephens Green Shopping Centre truly is 'The Shopping Centre of Dublin'.

Destination: Shopping

Stephen's Green
SHOPPING CENTRE
The Shopping Centre of Dublin

Rhinestones at 18 Andrew Street is home to a century of amazing costume jewellery, antique to modern reflecting art, fashion, history and romance. Walk through their door and you will experience a treasure trove of moments captured in time. From Early Victorian brooches, to romantic Edwardian keepsake lockets, to exquisite Venetian glass beads, to one-off 1960's studio silver creations. Selected Arts and Crafts items. European and American designer jewellery from the 1930's such as Miriam Haskell, Trifari, Dior. etc. Rhinestones also has a great range of new cultured pearl jewellery.

Carroll's Irish Gifts and Souvenirs are a fully Irish owned company established in 1982 and are one of the leading retailers of quality Irish sport and fashion clothing, souvenirs and gift products. They have many locations in Dublin including Westmoreland Street, 33 Lower O' Connell Street, Suffolk Street, 57/58 O' Connell Street, Henry Street and Talbot Street and stock many leading Irish brands such as FAI, Guinness, and Inis fragrances.

Temple Bar is now one of the most visited areas in the city and is widely regarded as the 'trendy' part of town; its selection of alternative clothes and record stores confirms this.

Celtic Designs is Dublin's newest Irish Craft and gift boutique shop, situated in the heart of Dublin's cultural quarter, Temple Bar. They feature a range of Irish Celtic and Claddagh Jewellery to suit every style, occasion and budget and stock only the best of Irish crafts and Irish Gifts. The crafters they work with are both guaranteed Irish and supported by the craft council of Ireland.

And on to **Henry Street**, the hunting ground of the sales fanatic. This area has undergone a costly facelift in recent years, attracting many new businesses and it now rivals Grafton Street as Dublin's favourite shopping venue. With UK stores such as **Marks & Spencer, Debenhams** and **Boots** all present, be careful not to overlook the many Irish department stores such as – **Arnotts** – which could tempt the last euro out of your pocket.

Extending off Henry Street are the **Jervis Street** and **Ilac Shopping Centres**, both which offer an exciting and varied shopping experience under one roof. Walking back towards the Spire brings you on to O'Connell Street, where **Clerys Department Store** and **Eason Bookshop** stand as Dublin institutions.

The Ilac Shopping Centre on Henry Street in Dublin's city centre is open seven days a week. Home to over 80 stores, the centre boasts over 28 fashion and accessory outlets and 13 eateries. Just some of the shops you may wish to visit include Angel, Diesel, Tierneys, Champion Sports, Debenhams and Dunnes Stores. For a bite to eat try Quigley's or O' Briens.

If you want to sample some shopping outside of the city centre, large suburban shopping malls have sprung up around Dublin in recent years, most notably: **Dundrum**

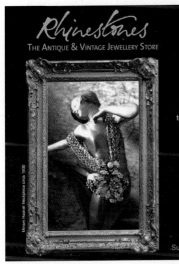

Towncentre, Liffey Valley, the Blanchardstown Centre and **The Square** in Tallaght. In general, shopping hours are 9am to 6pm, Monday to Saturday, with late opening on Thursdays. City centre shops are usually open between 12pm and 6pm on Sundays.

With 120 stores over 3 levels **Dundrum Town Centre** boasts Southern Ireland's only Harvey Nichols luxe boutique department store, House of Fraser department store over 4 floors, Hamleys Toy Store, Massimo Dutti, Hollister along with High Street names such as Marks & Spencer, Penney's, River Island, Zara, H & M and Next. Covered car parking services every level of the shopping mall. Dundrum is extremely well serviced by public transport with the Luas Green Line stopping just 150 metres away from the centre. Whatever the weather Dundrum Town Centre has you covered.

Blanchardstown Centre offers a unique shopping & leisure experience. Home to over 180 stores, 3 Retail Parks and 25 Restaurants, it is located just outside Dublin City on the N3, (M50 exit 6) linked to all major motorways making it Ireland's most accessible and largest destination shopping centre. Parking is completely free. Shopping is a pleasure at Blanchardstown Centre with over 180 stores to choose from including Debenhams, Marks & Spencer, BT2, French Connection, H&M, Topshop, River Island, Oasis, Warehouse, Zara, Superdry, Parfois, Dunnes Stores & Penneys. For more information visit www.blanchardstowncentre.com.

For shopping outside Dublin, we highly recommend **The Kildare Village**, one of the Collection of nine Chic Outlet Shopping Villages in Europe. Some of the brands here include Juicy Couture, DKNY, Cath Kidston, Jack Willis, Ted Baker, Calvin Klein and Hugo Boss. After your day of shopping and browsing, relax with a coffee in Starbucks and go for a snack in Crêperie Amélie.

The Ilac Centre is home to over 80 stores including names such as Debenhams, Dunnes Stores, TK Maxx, River Island, H&M, Argos and Jack & Jones as well as a host of boutique fashion retailers, jewellers, hair and beauty salons, gift shops and lots of places to eat including favourites such as Starbucks, Sbarro Pizza, McDonalds & Burger King.

Centrally situated in Dublin's premier shopping precinct, Henry Street, the Ilac has entrances from Moore Street and Parnell Street as well as Henry Street.

Close to the Garden of Remembrance, where Queen Elizabeth visited in 2011, to Moore Street with its famous market and 1916 monuments, the Spire, the Hugh Lane Gallery of Modern and Contemporary Art and the Writers' Museum you will also find two superb restaurants nearby: the renowned Chapter One Restaurant and the Hot Stove Restaurant both around the corner in Parnell Square. The Gate Theatre, the magnificent Rotunda Hospital, the Gresham Hotel, the GPO, the Leprechaun Museum, and The Church Café, Bar & Restaurant in Mary Street where Arthur Guinness was married and many other historic sites and buildings are also in this historic area.

The Ilac offers quality, variety and value in gifts, fashion, footwear, accessories and homewares. A visit to Dublin wouldn't be complete without a visit to the Ilac Centre.

Located within 5 minutes' walk from O'Connell Street the Ilac Centre is close to bus stops, Dublin Bike stations, Luas, Dart and Taxi ranks and it has a 1,000 space car park from only €2 per hour.

Open Mon-Wed 9am-6.30pm, Thurs 9am-9pm, Fri/Sat 9am-7pm and Sun11 am-6.30pm.

Find us, Like us and Follow us on www.ilac.ie, Facebook.com/IlacShoppingCentre and on Twitter @IlacCentre.

ilac
SHOPPING

BLANCHARDSTOWN CENTRE
Dublin 15
Tel: 01 822 1356
Email: info@blanchardstowncentre.com
Web: www.blanchardstowncentre.com

Blanchardstown Centre is Ireland's most accessible and largest destination shopping centre. Home to over 180 stores, 3 Retail Parks and 25 Restaurants, located just outside Dublin City on the N3, (M50 exit 6) linked to all major motorways and Parking is completely free.

CELTIC WHISKEY SHOP & WINES ON THE GREEN
27-28 Dawson Street, Dublin 2
Tel: +353 1 6759744
Email: ally@celticwhiskeyshop.com
Web: www.celticwhiskeyshop.com
www.winesonthegreen.com
Follow us on Twitter: @Celticwhiskey
@winesonthegreen
Online Ordering Available.

International Shipping Available. Welcome to Ireland's whiskey specialist, stocking the largest and finest selection of Irish, Scottish & world whiskeys, rare bottlings & miniatures. We offer free in store tastings daily. Also stocking a broad & eclectic range of competitively priced Wines, Champagnes, Irish Ales and Handmade Irish Chocolates.

ILAC SHOPPING CENTRE
Henry Street,
Dublin 1
Tel: 00353 (0)1 828 8900
Email: info@ilac.ie
Web: www.ilac.ie

The Ilac Centre, in the heart of Dublin, is home to over 80 stores including Debenhams, Dunnes Stores, River Island, TK Maxx, H&M and Argos. It has over 13 cafés including Starbucks. Accessible by bus, Dart, and Luas the Ilac also has a 1,000 space car park with parking from only €2 per hour*.
*rate applicable at time of going to print

KILDARE VILLAGE CHIC OUTLET SHOPPING
Nurney Road,
Kildare Town,
Co Kildare
Tel: +353 (0)45 520 501
Email: KildareVillage@ValueRetail.com
Web: www.KildareVillage.com

For a great day out, nestled within landscaped grounds and presented in an authentic village environment, Kildare Village is Ireland's luxury outlet shopping destination. You will find it difficult to resist temptation with your favourite designer brands such as Anya Hindmarch, Brooks Brothers, Coach, Furla, Links of London and N.Peal offering up to 60% off all year round.

NEW MOON
28 Drury st, George st Arcade, Dublin 2
Tel: 01 6711154
Email: info@newmoon.ie
Web: www.newmoon.ie
Also on Facebook: New Moon Jewellery

New Moon has Ireland's largest range of handmade silver, gold and natural gemstone jewellery from around the world, all ethically sourced. Topaz, opal, aquamarine, moonstone, amber, turquoise & many more. Women's & men's jewellery, rings, pendants, bracelets, cufflinks. A must for jewellery lovers.

POWERSCOURT TOWNHOUSE CENTRE
59 South William Street,
Dublin 2
Tel (01) 6794144 (Information Desk) & 01 6717000 (Office)
web: www.powerscourtcentre.com

Step inside Powerscourt Townhouse Centre, minutes from Grafton Street, and discover much more than a shopping centre.... Built in the eighteenth century it houses over 40 shops & places to eat. You'll find art, antique galleries and markets showcasing Irish Designers. ATM. Disabled access.

RHINESTONES
18 St Andrew St. Dublin 2
Tel: 00 353 01 6790759
Web: www.rhinestones.ie

Rhinestones specialist, antique and vintage popular jewellery of the 1800's,1900's to today. A vast selection of Venetian and Bohemian glass beads, Irish bog oak, Hollywood inspired rhinestone jewellery and much much more. Our Friendly and helpful staff will advise on the age, materials used, country of origin, etc.

STEPHEN'S GREEN SHOPPING CENTRE
St Stephen's Green West,
Dublin 2
Tel: 00 353 1 4780888
Fax: 00 353 1 4782565
Email: info@stephensgreen.com
Web: www.stephensgreen.com

Stephen's Green S.C. centrally located in the heart of Dublin's prestigious shopping area, surrounded by history and the hustle and bustle of Grafton Street. With over 100 outlets, a visit is a must for any visitor to the Dublin City.

THE KILKENNY SHOP
6-15 Nassau Street,
Dublin 2
Tel: 01 677 7066
Email: info@kilkennygroup.com
Web: www.kilkennyshop.com

The beautiful Kilkenny Shop is famous for promoting Irish design and crafts for over 50 years – located opposite Trinity College it's must see while in Dublin. Offering Waterford crystal, pottery, linen, jewellery, fashion, accessories and souvenirs. Tax free shopping & shipping promotions.

THE SWEATER SHOP
30 Nassau Street,
Tel: 01 671 2292
Email: sales@sweatershop.ie
Website: www.sweatershop.com

The Sweater Shop is a family run business & has been renowned for 30 years by locals & visitors alike. It stocks the largest collection of Irish quality knitwear for Ladies, Gents and Children, all at reasonable prices. Its flagship store is located in the heart of the city on Nassau Street, Dublin opposite Trinity College.

SPORT & RECREATION
Gaelic Games
Gaelic Games, which are indigenous to the Irish, are Ireland's national sports and a must–see for any tourist. For a good day out, catch a Gaelic Football match (think soccer, but using your hands as well as your feet), or a game of Hurling (like aerial hockey and reputedly the fastest field game in the world). Many games are held at Croke Park, now one of Europe's largest stadiums, with a capacity in excess of 80,000.

Rugby
There are many rugby clubs in Dublin but the centre of attention each season is always Leinster, the professional provincial side which has had outstanding success in recent years in the Heineken European Cup. Leinster matches are played at the RDS and more recently at the Aviva Stadium in Landsdowne Road both on the south side of the city.

Horse Racing
Leopardstown, in South County Dublin, is one of Ireland's most modern racetracks, while to the northwest of the city, in County Meath, Fairyhouse is home of the Irish Grand National. In **Kildare**, the Curragh plays host to the annual Irish Derby. Naas and Punchestown racecourses are also nearby and can be easily reached by exiting the M7 motorway.

LISTINGS

SHELBOURNE PARK GREYHOUND STADIUM
South Lotts Road, Ringsend, Dublin 4
Tel: 1890-269-969
Fax: 01 6683246
Email: sales@igb.ie
Web:www.shelbourneparkgreyhoundstadium.ie

A perfect location whatever the occasion be it a family or work outing, Corporate event or simply a night out with friends. Racing every Wednesday, Thursday and Saturday (additional Friday nights racing in December). Packages available to suit all budgets.
For reservations call 1890 269 969.

STEPASIDE GOLF CENTRE
Jamestown Farm, Kilternan, Dublin 18
Tel: 01-2953326 / 01-2149638
Fax: 01-2957204
Email: stepasidegolf@eircom.net
Web: www.stepasidegolfcentre.ie

Stepaside Golf Centre is nestled in the foothills of the Dublin Mountains.
Golfers have the most beautiful backdrop to their Practice Session & Par 3 Game. Located on the Enniskerry Road South of Stepaside Village, we are easily accessible from the City Centre & M50 motorway via junctions 13, 14 & 15.

Greyhound Racing

Also popular is Greyhound Racing, at **Shelbourne Park** Greyhound Stadium with races every Wednesday, Thursday and Saturday where you can be sure to enjoy a great night of hospitality, excitement and sporting action. Shelbourne Park is just a fifteen minute walk from Dublin city centre. **Harold's Cross** is also a superb purpose built facility guaranteeing a fun night out.

Golf

With six championship courses and eleven links, Dublin is an excellent base for your golfing holiday. A visit to Portmarnock Links, Royal Dublin Golf Links and The Island Golf Club amongst others are well–recommended.

Stepaside Golf Centre has served as one of Ireland's top golf practice and tuition centres, providing golfers of all abilities and ages with an opportunity & facilities to develop their game of golf. The golf centre is nestled in the foothills of the Dublin Mountains. Facilities include 40 bay floodlit driving range, 18–hole, par 3 golf course, PGA approved teaching centre & coffee shop.

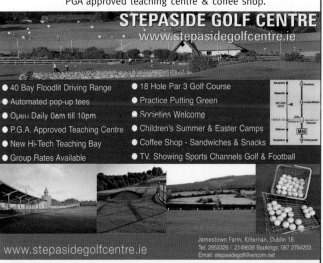

DART Commuter Rail Network
Visit irishrail.ie for travel information

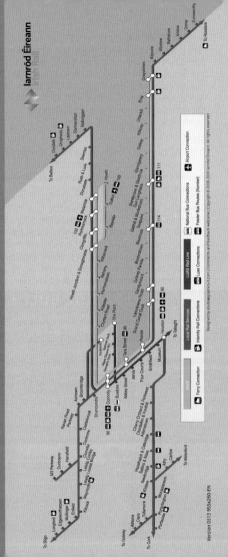

Version 0513 955x260-EN